I0503716

The Secure Coder's Handbook

A Practical Guide to Secure Development

Jack Davies

Welcome to "The Secure Coder's Handbook: A Practical Guide to Secure Development." In today's digital landscape, where technology is deeply intertwined with our personal and professional lives, security has become paramount. The impact of insecure coding practices can be far-reaching, leading to data breaches, system vulnerabilities, financial losses, and damage to reputations. As developers, it is our responsibility to build robust and secure software that protects sensitive information, safeguards user privacy, and ensures the reliability of our applications.

This handbook is designed as a comprehensive guide to help developers, engineers, and software professionals embrace secure coding principles and best practices throughout the development lifecycle. Whether you are an experienced programmer or just starting your journey in software development, this book will equip you with the knowledge and tools needed to write secure code and mitigate potential risks.

Chapter 1 provides a foundational understanding of secure development. We delve into the importance of secure coding practices, emphasizing the need to shift our mindset from treating security as an afterthought to integrating it as an inherent part of the development process. By comprehending the impact of insecure code on applications and systems, we can better appreciate the urgency and significance of implementing secure coding practices.

In Chapter 2, we explore the core principles and best practices of secure coding. From input validation and output encoding to proper error handling, we will examine techniques that help fortify our code against common vulnerabilities such as injection attacks, buffer overflows, and cross-site scripting. Additionally, we will delve into secure coding standards and frameworks that provide guidelines for maintaining code integrity and security.

Effective threat modeling and risk assessment are crucial steps in developing secure software. Chapter 3 guides us through the process of identifying potential security risks and analyzing their impact and likelihood. By prioritizing and mitigating risks based on the specific context of our development projects, we can allocate resources more effectively and proactively address potential vulnerabilities.

Authentication and authorization mechanisms are essential components of secure applications. In Chapter 4, we explore the design and implementation of secure authentication systems. We will examine techniques such as multi-factor authentication, biometrics, and secure session management to ensure that only authorized individuals can access sensitive resources. By understanding various authorization models, including role-based and attribute-based access control, we can implement robust access control mechanisms.

Chapter 5 focuses on securing data throughout its lifecycle. We explore encryption and hashing techniques for secure data storage and transmission, as well as best practices for securely storing sensitive information in databases, files, and other storage mediums. By employing encryption and secure communication protocols, we can protect data from unauthorized access and ensure its confidentiality and integrity.

Web applications are particularly vulnerable to attacks due to their exposed nature. Chapter 6 delves into the specific security considerations for web development. We examine common web application vulnerabilities, such as cross-site scripting (XSS) and cross-site request forgery (CSRF), and discuss techniques to defend against these threats. By implementing secure coding practices specific to web applications, we can minimize the risk of exploitation and protect user data.

Lastly, Chapter 7 explores secure development practices for mobile and IoT applications. With the proliferation of smartphones and connected devices, securing mobile and IoT applications has become paramount. We discuss the unique challenges and vulnerabilities associated with these platforms and delve into best practices for securing data storage, network communication, and firmware development.

Throughout this handbook, we provide practical examples, code snippets, and real-world scenarios to illustrate the concepts and techniques discussed. Our aim is to empower you with the knowledge and skills to write secure code from the ground up. By implementing the principles and practices outlined in this handbook, you will be better equipped to protect your applications, users, and organizations from the ever-evolving landscape of cyber threats.

Remember, security is not a one-time endeavor but an ongoing commitment. By adopting a proactive and security-conscious mindset, we can collectively build a safer digital ecosystem. Let "The Secure Coder's Handbook: A Practical Guide to Secure Development" be your companion in this journey towards becoming a confident and responsible secure coder.

Happy coding and secure development!

Sincerely,
Jack Davies

Chapter 1: Introduction to Secure Development

Welcome to Chapter 1 of "The Secure Coder's Handbook: A Practical Guide to Secure Development." In this chapter, we embark on a journey to explore the foundations of secure development and understand the importance of integrating security into the development process.

In today's digital age, where technology permeates every aspect of our lives, security breaches and vulnerabilities have become an all-too-common occurrence. The consequences of insecure code can be catastrophic, resulting in data breaches, financial losses, compromised user privacy, and damage to an organization's reputation. As developers, it is our responsibility to build software that not only delivers functionality but also prioritizes the security and integrity of the systems we create.

In this introductory chapter, we aim to instill a security-conscious mindset and provide a holistic view of secure development. We begin by exploring the significance of secure coding practices and the reasons why they should be an integral part of our development workflows from the outset.

To fully grasp the importance of secure development, it is essential to understand the potential impact of insecure code on applications and systems. From data leakage and unauthorized access to system crashes and manipulation of critical operations, the consequences can be far-reaching. By recognizing these risks, we can better appreciate the urgency and significance of implementing secure coding practices.

Throughout this chapter, we will also delve into the concept of security vulnerabilities. We will explore common security flaws and the implications they can have on software applications. By understanding the various types of vulnerabilities, such as injection attacks, cross-site scripting, and buffer overflows, we can gain insights into how and why they occur. This knowledge will serve as a foundation for the subsequent chapters, where we will explore specific techniques to mitigate these vulnerabilities.

Moreover, we will discuss the evolution of the development landscape and how the rise of interconnected systems, cloud computing, and mobile applications has presented new challenges and risks. As technology advances, so do the methods employed by attackers. Therefore, we must adapt our development practices to address these emerging threats proactively.

At the heart of secure development lies the concept of shifting from a reactive approach to a proactive one. Rather than addressing security as an afterthought, secure coding necessitates a mindset that prioritizes security considerations throughout the entire development lifecycle. By integrating security into the early stages of planning, design, coding, testing, and deployment, we can significantly reduce the likelihood of security vulnerabilities and minimize their potential impact.

In the subsequent chapters, we will dive deeper into the practical aspects of secure development. We will explore secure coding principles, best practices, and techniques that can be employed to fortify our code against common vulnerabilities. We will also delve into threat modeling and risk assessment, authentication and authorization mechanisms, secure data storage and transmission, securing web applications, and developing secure mobile and IoT applications.

By the end of this handbook, you will have gained the knowledge, tools, and confidence to become a secure coder. You will be equipped with a comprehensive understanding of secure development practices and the ability to apply them effectively in your day-to-day work.

So, let us embark on this journey together, laying a solid foundation for secure coding practices. By embracing the principles and techniques outlined in this chapter and throughout the book, we can contribute to a safer and more secure digital landscape. Together, let us build robust, trustworthy, and resilient software applications.

1.1 The Importance of Secure Coding

Secure coding is an essential aspect of software development that aims to create applications that are resistant to malicious attacks and vulnerabilities. In today's interconnected and digitized world, where cyber threats are prevalent, secure coding practices have become more critical than ever. This section explores the importance of secure coding and its impact on the overall security posture of software applications.

1.1.1 Mitigating Security Risks

Secure coding practices play a fundamental role in mitigating security risks associated with software development. By adhering to secure coding principles, developers can minimize the likelihood of introducing vulnerabilities that could be exploited by attackers. Common security risks, such as injection attacks, cross-site scripting (XSS), and broken authentication, can be effectively mitigated through proper coding techniques.

For example, the use of input validation and output encoding can prevent injection attacks by ensuring that user input is sanitized and properly handled.

Similarly, implementing secure authentication and session management mechanisms can significantly reduce the risk of unauthorized access and session-related vulnerabilities. By following secure coding practices, developers can proactively address security risks and build resilient applications.

1.1.2 Protecting Sensitive Data

Data breaches and unauthorized access to sensitive information pose significant threats to individuals and organizations. Secure coding practices help protect sensitive data by implementing robust security measures throughout the application's lifecycle. Encryption techniques, secure storage mechanisms, and secure transmission protocols ensure that sensitive data is protected both at rest and in transit.

By properly handling and securing sensitive data, developers can maintain the confidentiality and integrity of user information, such as personally identifiable information (PII) and financial data. This not only safeguards individuals' privacy but also helps organizations comply with data protection regulations and build trust with their users.

1.1.3 Building Trust and Reputation

Security breaches and vulnerabilities can have severe consequences for organizations, including reputational damage and loss of customer trust.

Secure coding practices demonstrate a commitment to security and the protection of user data. By prioritizing security during the development process, organizations can instill confidence in their customers and stakeholders.

Customers are increasingly aware of the importance of security, and they expect the applications they use to prioritize their data protection. By incorporating secure coding practices, organizations can differentiate themselves from competitors and establish a reputation for providing secure and trustworthy applications. This trust and reputation are vital for attracting and retaining customers in today's competitive landscape.

1.1.4 Reducing Costs and Liabilities

Addressing security issues during the development phase is more cost-effective than addressing them after a security breach or vulnerability is exploited. By investing in secure coding practices from the beginning, organizations can save substantial costs associated with remediating security incidents, conducting forensic investigations, and recovering from reputational damage.

Additionally, secure coding practices help minimize legal liabilities that may arise from security breaches. Data protection regulations, such as the General Data Protection Regulation (GDPR), impose significant penalties for non-compliance and mishandling of personal data. By integrating security into the development process, organizations can mitigate the risk of non-compliance and potential legal consequences.

1.1.5 Ensuring Long-Term Application Security

Secure coding is not a one-time effort but an ongoing process. Applications need to adapt to emerging threats and evolving security standards. By adopting secure coding practices, organizations can establish a foundation for long-term application security. Regular code reviews, vulnerability assessments, and security testing help identify and address security weaknesses, ensuring that applications remain resilient to new and emerging threats.

Moreover, incorporating security as an integral part of the development lifecycle promotes a security-conscious culture within the organization. It encourages developers to prioritize security and continually update their knowledge and skills to stay ahead of potential vulnerabilities.

In conclusion, secure coding is of utmost importance in software development. It helps mitigate security risks, protect sensitive data, build trust and reputation, reduce costs and liabilities, and ensure long-term application security. By embracing secure coding practices, organizations can enhance the security posture of their applications, protect user data, comply with regulations, and safeguard their reputation. Secure coding is not an option but a necessity in today's threat landscape, where cyberattacks continue to pose significant risks.

1.2 Impact of Insecure Code on Applications and Systems

Insecure code can have a detrimental impact on the security and functionality of applications and systems. It exposes vulnerabilities that can be exploited by attackers, leading to various consequences ranging from data breaches to system compromise. This section highlights the significant impact of insecure code and emphasizes the importance of secure coding practices in mitigating these risks.

1.2.1 Data Breaches and Unauthorized Access

Insecure code can result in data breaches and unauthorized access to sensitive information. Vulnerabilities such as SQL injection, cross-site scripting (XSS), and insecure authentication mechanisms can be exploited by attackers to gain unauthorized access to databases, manipulate data, or steal sensitive information. These breaches can have severe consequences, including financial loss, reputational damage, and legal liabilities.

By exploiting insecure code, attackers can access personally identifiable information (PII), financial data, or confidential business information. The impact of a data breach can be far-reaching, affecting not only the individuals whose data has been compromised but also the organization responsible for safeguarding that data. Secure coding practices, including input validation, output encoding, and secure authentication mechanisms, are essential in preventing these vulnerabilities and protecting sensitive data.

1.2.2 System Compromise and Control

Insecure code can allow attackers to gain control over applications and systems, leading to system compromise. By exploiting vulnerabilities such as remote code execution or privilege escalation, attackers can execute arbitrary code on servers or devices, manipulate system configurations, or gain administrative access. Once in control, attackers can use the compromised systems as a foothold for further attacks, install malicious software, or launch attacks against other systems.

System compromise can disrupt business operations, cause downtime, and result in the loss of critical data. It can also enable attackers to conduct further malicious activities, such as launching distributed denial-of-service (DDoS) attacks or spreading malware. Secure coding practices, such as secure input handling, secure configuration management, and secure coding libraries, help prevent these vulnerabilities and reduce the risk of system compromise.

1.2.3 Loss of Service Availability

Insecure code can lead to service disruptions and the loss of availability for applications and systems. Vulnerabilities such as buffer overflows, race conditions, or resource exhaustion can cause applications to crash, hang, or become unresponsive. These vulnerabilities can be exploited by attackers or inadvertently triggered by legitimate user actions, resulting in service interruptions and negative user experiences.

The loss of service availability can have significant consequences, especially for critical systems or online services that rely on uninterrupted operation. It can result in financial losses, damage to reputation, and loss of customer trust. By following secure coding practices, including proper memory management, concurrency control, and resource allocation, developers can minimize the risk of these vulnerabilities and ensure the availability of their applications and systems.

1.2.4 Escalation of Privileges and Lateral Movement

Insecure code can enable attackers to escalate their privileges within an application or system and move laterally through the network. Vulnerabilities such as insecure session management, insecure access control, or inadequate input validation can be exploited to gain unauthorized privileges or bypass security controls. Once attackers gain elevated privileges, they can move laterally through the network, accessing sensitive resources, and potentially compromising additional systems.

Privilege escalation and lateral movement can lead to further compromise of critical systems, unauthorized access to sensitive data, and the potential for persistent control within an organization's network. Secure coding practices, including robust access control mechanisms, proper session management, and input validation, are crucial in preventing these vulnerabilities and limiting the impact of potential attacks.

In conclusion, insecure code can have severe consequences for applications and systems, including data breaches, system compromise, loss of service availability, and unauthorized access. The impact of these vulnerabilities can be far-reaching, affecting individuals, organizations, and even the broader ecosystem. By prioritizing secure coding practices, organizations can mitigate these risks, protect their applications and systems, and ensure the confidentiality, integrity, and availability of their data.

1.3 Common Security Vulnerabilities and Their Consequences

Software applications are susceptible to various security vulnerabilities that can be exploited by attackers to compromise the confidentiality, integrity, and availability of data. Understanding these vulnerabilities is crucial for developers to effectively mitigate risks and build secure applications. This section highlights some of the most common security vulnerabilities and their potential consequences.

1.3.1 Injection Attacks

Injection attacks, such as SQL injection and command injection, occur when untrusted data is inserted into an application's code without proper validation or sanitization. Attackers can exploit these vulnerabilities to execute malicious commands or inject malicious code into an application's backend database or operating system.

Consequences:

- Unauthorized access to sensitive data stored in databases
- Data manipulation or destruction
- Full compromise of the application or system

- Exposure of user credentials or personal information

1.3.2 Cross-Site Scripting (XSS)

Cross-Site Scripting (XSS) vulnerabilities allow attackers to inject malicious scripts into web pages viewed by other users. These scripts can be used to steal sensitive information, hijack user sessions, or deface websites.

Consequences:

- Theft of sensitive user information (e.g., login credentials, payment details)
- Hijacking of user sessions
- Defacement or manipulation of website content
- Distribution of malware to unsuspecting users

1.3.3 Cross-Site Request Forgery (CSRF)

Cross-Site Request Forgery (CSRF) vulnerabilities enable attackers to execute unauthorized actions on behalf of authenticated users. By tricking users into unknowingly performing actions on a vulnerable website, attackers can manipulate user data or perform malicious operations.

Consequences:

- Unauthorized modification or deletion of user data
- Unauthorized actions performed on behalf of users (e.g., changing account settings, making financial transactions)
- Potential exposure of sensitive information

1.3.4 Broken Authentication and Session Management

Weaknesses in authentication and session management mechanisms can expose user accounts to unauthorized access. Attackers can exploit these vulnerabilities to impersonate legitimate users, bypass authentication controls, or hijack user sessions.

Consequences:

- Unauthorized access to user accounts
- Theft of sensitive user information or personal data
- Unauthorized actions performed on behalf of legitimate users
- Compromise of user privacy and confidentiality

1.3.5 Insecure Direct Object References

Insecure Direct Object References occur when an application exposes internal references (such as database keys or file paths) without proper authorization checks. Attackers can exploit these vulnerabilities to access and manipulate sensitive data directly.

Consequences:

- Unauthorized access to sensitive data or resources
- Modification or deletion of sensitive data
- Exposure of confidential information

1.3.6 Security Misconfigurations

Security misconfigurations arise from the improper configuration of software components, servers, frameworks, or platforms. These misconfigurations can lead to unintended exposure of sensitive information or the presence of default or weak security settings.

Consequences:

- Unauthorized access to sensitive data or resources
- Exploitation of default credentials or weak configurations
- Increased attack surface and potential compromise of the entire system

1.3.7 Denial-of-Service (DoS) Attacks

Denial-of-Service (DoS) attacks aim to disrupt or disable the availability of an application or system by overwhelming it with excessive requests or consuming its resources. These attacks can be achieved through various means, such as network-based flooding or resource exhaustion.

Consequences:

- Disruption of service availability
- Loss of user trust and confidence
- Financial losses due to business interruption
- Potential exploitation of other vulnerabilities during system overload

Understanding these common security vulnerabilities and their potential consequences is vital for developers to design and implement effective mitigation measures. By following secure coding practices, conducting thorough vulnerability assessments, and adopting robust security controls, developers can significantly reduce the risk of exploitation and build more secure applications.

1.4: The Evolution of Secure Development

Secure development practices have evolved significantly over time in response to the ever-increasing threats and challenges in the digital landscape. This section explores the evolution of secure development, highlighting key milestones and shifts in mindset that have shaped the way we approach security in software development.

1.4.1 Reactive Approach

In the early days of software development, security was often an afterthought. Developers focused primarily on functionality and speed, neglecting security considerations. As a result, applications were riddled with vulnerabilities, and security breaches were commonplace.

The reactive approach to security involved addressing security issues only after they were discovered or exploited. Organizations would react to incidents by patching vulnerabilities or applying quick fixes. However, this approach was inherently flawed, as it did not address the root causes of vulnerabilities and often led to a cat-and-mouse game with attackers.

1.4.2 Shift to Proactive Security

Recognizing the shortcomings of the reactive approach, the industry began shifting towards a more proactive stance on security. This shift involved integrating security into the software development lifecycle from the outset. Developers started considering security requirements, conducting risk assessments, and implementing security controls during the development process.

Secure coding practices and security-focused development frameworks emerged, emphasizing the importance of validating input, sanitizing data, and implementing secure authentication and access control mechanisms. The goal was to identify and mitigate security risks early in the development lifecycle, reducing the likelihood of introducing vulnerabilities.

1.4.3 Rise of Secure Development Frameworks and Standards

To further promote secure development practices, industry-standard frameworks and guidelines were developed. These frameworks, such as the Open Web Application Security Project (OWASP) Top Ten, provide developers with a set of best practices and recommendations for addressing common security vulnerabilities.

Secure coding standards, such as CERT Secure Coding Standards, were established to define secure coding practices across different programming languages. These standards serve as a reference for developers, guiding them in writing secure code and avoiding common pitfalls.

1.4.4 Integration of Security Testing

As secure development practices matured, the integration of security testing became a crucial aspect of the development process. Static Application Security Testing (SAST) and Dynamic Application Security Testing (DAST) tools were introduced to identify vulnerabilities during the development and testing phases.

Automated vulnerability scanning and code analysis tools helped developers identify security weaknesses and receive actionable feedback to remediate them. The shift towards DevSecOps, the integration of security practices into DevOps workflows, further emphasized the importance of continuous security testing throughout the development lifecycle.

1.4.5 Embracing Secure Development Frameworks

To streamline secure development practices, organizations started adopting secure development frameworks and methodologies. These frameworks provide a structured approach to developing secure applications by incorporating security activities into each phase of the development process.

One such framework is the Microsoft Secure Development Lifecycle (SDL), which outlines security activities, guidelines, and requirements for each stage of development. By following frameworks like SDL, organizations can establish consistent security practices, reducing the risk of vulnerabilities and ensuring the overall security of their applications.

1.4.6 Shift to Secure-by-Design Approach

The latest evolution in secure development is the shift towards a secure-by-design approach. This approach advocates for integrating security as a fundamental aspect of the software design process itself. By considering security requirements and constraints at the design stage, developers can build applications with inherent security measures.

Secure-by-design emphasizes the use of secure coding patterns, secure architecture principles, and threat modeling techniques to identify and address security risks proactively. It promotes a security-first mindset, where developers consider the potential impact of their design decisions on the overall security posture of the application.

In conclusion, secure development practices have evolved from a reactive approach to a proactive, security-focused mindset. With the integration of secure coding practices, standardized frameworks, security testing, and a secure-by-design approach, developers are better equipped to build resilient and secure applications. As the threat landscape continues to evolve, the ongoing evolution of secure development practices remains essential to stay ahead of emerging threats and protect digital assets effectively.

1.5: The Secure Development Lifecycle

The Secure Development Lifecycle (SDL) is a systematic and structured approach to software development that integrates security practices throughout the entire development process. By incorporating security from the early stages of design to the deployment and maintenance phases, the SDL aims to build secure and resilient applications. This section explores the key stages of the Secure Development Lifecycle and highlights their significance in ensuring secure software development.

1.5.1 Requirements Gathering and Analysis

The first stage of the SDL involves gathering and analyzing security requirements. This includes identifying potential threats, defining security objectives, and determining regulatory and compliance requirements. By understanding the security needs of the application, developers can align their development efforts to meet those requirements.

During this stage, threat modeling is often conducted to identify potential vulnerabilities and assess the risks associated with the application. This helps in making informed decisions about security controls and countermeasures that should be implemented throughout the development process.

1.5.2 Design and Architecture

In the design and architecture phase, developers create the blueprint for the application's structure, functionality, and security features. Security considerations, such as secure coding practices, secure communication protocols, and access control mechanisms, are incorporated into the design.

Threat modeling continues during this stage to refine the understanding of potential risks and guide the design decisions. The goal is to create a robust and secure architecture that can withstand potential attacks and protect sensitive data.

1.5.3 Secure Coding and Implementation

Secure coding practices play a pivotal role in the secure development lifecycle. Developers must follow coding guidelines and best practices to minimize the introduction of vulnerabilities. This includes input validation, output encoding, secure error handling, and secure use of APIs and libraries.

By adhering to secure coding practices, developers can mitigate common vulnerabilities, such as injection attacks, cross-site scripting (XSS), and insecure direct object references. Code reviews and automated static analysis tools can also be used to identify and remediate security issues before they manifest in the final product.

1.5.4 Testing and Quality Assurance

Testing and quality assurance are critical stages in the secure development lifecycle. In addition to functional testing, security testing is performed to identify vulnerabilities and validate the effectiveness of implemented security controls.

Different types of security testing, such as penetration testing, vulnerability scanning, and security code reviews, are conducted to uncover vulnerabilities and assess the application's resilience against attacks. Test results are analyzed, and necessary remediation steps are taken to address identified security weaknesses.

1.5.5 Deployment and Maintenance

The deployment and maintenance phase involves ensuring the secure deployment of the application and maintaining its security posture over time. This includes securely configuring servers and environments, applying patches and updates, and monitoring the application for security incidents.

Ongoing security assessments, such as periodic vulnerability scanning and security audits, are performed to identify any new vulnerabilities or changes in the threat landscape. Incident response plans and procedures are established to address security incidents promptly and effectively.

1.5.6 Training and Awareness

The Secure Development Lifecycle also emphasizes the importance of training and awareness among developers and stakeholders. Security education programs and training sessions help developers stay updated with the latest secure coding practices and emerging threats. By fostering a security-conscious culture, organizations can ensure that security is ingrained in the mindset of all individuals involved in the development process.

Regular security awareness programs for end-users and administrators also play a crucial role in maintaining the overall security of the application. Educating users about potential security risks, safe practices, and the importance of timely updates contributes to a more secure application ecosystem.

In conclusion, the Secure Development Lifecycle provides a framework for integrating security practices into every stage of the software development process. By adopting this holistic approach, organizations can build applications that are resilient to security threats, protect sensitive data, and maintain a strong security posture throughout their lifecycle.

1.6: The Role of the Secure Coder

In the context of secure development, the role of the secure coder is of paramount importance. Secure coders are developers who have a deep understanding of secure coding practices, vulnerabilities, and countermeasures. They play a crucial role in building robust and secure applications. This section explores the key responsibilities and skills of a secure coder and highlights the significance of their role in the development process.

1.6.1 Knowledge of Secure Coding Practices

A secure coder possesses a comprehensive understanding of secure coding practices. They are familiar with industry-standard coding guidelines, secure coding standards, and best practices for addressing common vulnerabilities. Secure coders follow principles such as input validation, output encoding, secure error handling, and secure use of cryptography to minimize the risk of introducing security vulnerabilities.

By applying their knowledge of secure coding practices, secure coders can prevent common vulnerabilities like injection attacks, cross-site scripting (XSS), and insecure direct object references. They actively seek to avoid coding practices that could compromise the security of the application.

1.6.2 Understanding of Security Vulnerabilities

Secure coders are well-versed in various security vulnerabilities and their underlying causes. They understand the techniques and methods employed by attackers to exploit vulnerabilities and compromise the security of applications. This knowledge enables them to anticipate potential risks and proactively implement appropriate security measures.

By understanding the nature and consequences of security vulnerabilities, secure coders can make informed design and implementation decisions. They actively consider potential attack vectors and implement countermeasures to protect the application against them.

1.6.3 Application of Security Controls

Secure coders are responsible for implementing security controls throughout the development process. This includes incorporating secure authentication and authorization mechanisms, implementing secure communication protocols, and employing secure data storage and transmission practices.

They leverage encryption, hashing, and other cryptographic techniques to protect sensitive data. They also consider security aspects when integrating third-party libraries and APIs, ensuring that they do not introduce additional vulnerabilities.

1.6.4 Collaboration with Security Professionals

Secure coders collaborate closely with security professionals, such as security architects, penetration testers, and security analysts. They work together to identify potential security risks, perform threat modeling, and validate the effectiveness of implemented security controls.

By collaborating with security professionals, secure coders gain valuable insights and expertise in identifying and addressing security vulnerabilities. This collaboration helps ensure that security considerations are integrated into the development process from the early stages and that potential risks are adequately mitigated.

1.6.5 Continuous Learning and Adaptation

The field of secure development is ever-evolving, with new vulnerabilities and attack techniques emerging regularly. Secure coders understand the importance of continuous learning and adaptation to stay updated with the latest security trends, technologies, and best practices.

They actively participate in security communities, attend relevant conferences and workshops, and engage in ongoing professional development. By staying informed about emerging threats and security advancements, secure coders can continuously enhance their skills and contribute to building more secure applications.

1.6.6 Promoting a Security Culture

Secure coders also play a vital role in promoting a security culture within development teams and organizations. They advocate for security as an essential aspect of software development and raise awareness among their peers about secure coding practices and potential security risks.

By fostering a security-conscious culture, secure coders contribute to creating an environment where security is prioritized throughout the development process. They encourage open communication, knowledge sharing, and collaboration to collectively improve the overall security posture of the organization.

In conclusion, the role of the secure coder is crucial in building secure applications. By possessing a deep understanding of secure coding practices, vulnerabilities, and countermeasures, secure coders contribute to mitigating security risks and protecting sensitive data. Their collaboration with security professionals, continuous learning, and promotion of a security culture are essential for developing applications with a strong security posture.

Chapter 2: Secure Coding Principles and Best Practices

Welcome to Chapter 2 of "The Secure Coder's Handbook: A Practical Guide to Secure Development." In this chapter, we delve into the core principles and best practices of secure coding. By adopting these principles and incorporating them into our development workflows, we can build software that is more resistant to security vulnerabilities and threats.

Secure coding begins with the understanding that all user inputs should be treated as potentially malicious. Input validation and sanitization are crucial techniques that help ensure the integrity and security of our applications. In this chapter, we explore the importance of input validation, discuss various input validation techniques, and provide practical examples of how to implement input validation effectively.

Output encoding and data validation are equally important aspects of secure coding. By properly encoding output, we can prevent common vulnerabilities such as cross-site scripting (XSS) attacks. We will delve into different encoding techniques and examine how they can be applied to sanitize output effectively. Additionally, we will discuss the significance of data validation, including validating user inputs, file uploads, and external data sources to prevent code injection and data manipulation attacks.

Error handling and logging are essential components of secure coding practices. Effective error handling not only improves the user experience but also plays a crucial role in identifying and mitigating security vulnerabilities. We will explore error handling techniques, including appropriate error messages, exception handling, and error logging. By implementing proper error handling and logging mechanisms, we can identify potential security issues and react proactively to them.

Secure configuration management is often overlooked but is a vital aspect of secure coding. In this chapter, we will discuss the importance of secure configuration management and explore techniques for securely managing configuration files, secrets, and credentials. We will also examine the significance of securely storing and managing sensitive information, such as API keys and database credentials, to prevent unauthorized access and reduce the risk of data breaches.

Adhering to secure coding standards and frameworks can significantly enhance the security of our code. In this chapter, we will discuss the importance of following established secure coding standards, such as the OWASP Top 10, CERT Coding Standards, and the MISRA C/C++ guidelines. These standards provide guidelines and best practices for writing secure code and help developers mitigate common vulnerabilities. We will also explore secure coding frameworks that offer ready-to-use libraries and functions to assist in secure development.

In conclusion, Chapter 2 equips us with the essential principles and best practices of secure coding. By implementing input validation, output encoding, proper error handling, secure configuration management, and adhering to secure coding standards, we build a solid foundation for developing secure software. These practices, when integrated into our development workflows, significantly reduce the risk of security vulnerabilities, ensuring that our applications are more resilient and less susceptible to attacks.

In the subsequent chapters, we will continue to explore specific aspects of secure development, including threat modeling and risk assessment, secure authentication and authorization mechanisms, securing data storage and transmission, securing web applications, and developing secure mobile and IoT applications. By combining these principles and practices, we will create a comprehensive understanding of secure development and become confident in our ability to write secure code.

So, let's delve deeper into the world of secure coding principles and best practices. By embracing these techniques, we can fortify our applications against potential security threats and contribute to a safer digital environment.

2.1 Input Validation and Sanitization

Input validation and sanitization are fundamental security practices that help prevent common vulnerabilities, such as injection attacks and cross-site scripting (XSS). This section explores the importance of input validation and sanitization, their role in preventing security vulnerabilities, and best practices for implementing these practices effectively.

2.1.1 Importance of Input Validation

Input validation is the process of validating and verifying user input to ensure it conforms to the expected format, type, and range. It is a critical security measure as malicious or malformed input can lead to various security vulnerabilities, including injection attacks, buffer overflows, and command execution.

By implementing robust input validation, developers can prevent attackers from exploiting vulnerabilities by injecting malicious code or unexpected input. Validating input at the earliest possible stage helps establish trust in the data and reduces the risk of security breaches.

2.1.2 Common Input Validation Techniques

There are several techniques and best practices for performing input validation effectively. Here are some commonly used approaches:

Whitelisting: Adopt a whitelist approach where input is validated against an explicitly defined set of allowed characters, formats, or patterns. This approach ensures that only expected and safe input is accepted.

Blacklisting: While less secure than whitelisting, blacklisting involves identifying and blocking known malicious input patterns. However, it is challenging to maintain an exhaustive list of all possible malicious inputs, making this approach less reliable.

Regular Expressions: Regular expressions can be used to define specific patterns that input must adhere to. This enables developers to perform more complex validation based on specific rules or formats.

Length and Range Checking: Validate the length and range of input to ensure it falls within acceptable limits. For example, if a user's age is required, ensure that the input is a positive integer within a reasonable range.

Data Type Validation: Verify that input matches the expected data type (e.g., string, integer, date) and handle type conversions appropriately.

2.1.3 Sanitization of User Input

Input sanitization involves removing or encoding potentially malicious or unwanted content from user input. While input validation focuses on checking if input meets expected criteria, sanitization is concerned with cleansing input to mitigate the risk of code injection and other security vulnerabilities.

Common sanitization techniques include:

HTML Encoding: Convert special characters to their respective HTML entities to prevent HTML and script injection attacks. This ensures that user input is treated as plain text and not interpreted as executable code by the browser.

SQL Parameterization: Use parameterized queries or prepared statements to separate data from the SQL query itself. This prevents SQL injection attacks by treating user input as data rather than executable SQL code.

File Path Sanitization: Ensure that user-supplied input for file paths or filenames is properly sanitized to prevent directory traversal attacks and unauthorized access to sensitive files.

Command Line Argument Sanitization: When executing system commands, validate and sanitize user input to prevent command injection attacks. Use platform-specific APIs or libraries that handle input validation and parameterization for command execution.

2.1.4 Validation and Sanitization in Web Applications

In the context of web applications, input validation and sanitization are of utmost importance. Web applications often rely on user input for various operations, making them vulnerable to attacks if not properly validated and sanitized.

Web frameworks and libraries often provide built-in mechanisms for input validation and sanitization. Developers should leverage these features to handle common security concerns effectively. Additionally, implementing server-side validation is crucial, as client-side validation alone can be bypassed or manipulated.

It is essential to validate and sanitize input at both the server-side and client-side. Client-side validation can improve user experience by providing immediate feedback, but it should never be relied upon as the sole means of security. Server-side validation acts as a final line of defense, ensuring that only valid and safe input is processed and acted upon.

2.1.5 Handling Validation Errors

When input validation fails, it is crucial to handle validation errors securely. Avoid exposing sensitive information in error messages, as this can provide valuable information to potential attackers. Instead, provide generic error messages that do not reveal specific details about the validation failure.

Logging validation errors can be useful for debugging and troubleshooting but ensure that sensitive information is not logged. Implement appropriate logging mechanisms and ensure that logs are properly secured and monitored to prevent information disclosure.

2.1.6 The Role of Automated Tools

Automated static analysis tools and vulnerability scanners can be valuable resources for identifying input validation and sanitization issues in codebases. These tools can help detect potential vulnerabilities and suggest improvements, but they should not be relied upon as the sole means of ensuring secure input handling. Manual code reviews and testing should always accompany the use of automated tools to provide a comprehensive security assessment.

In conclusion, input validation and sanitization are crucial practices for preventing common security vulnerabilities in software applications. By implementing robust validation techniques and effective sanitization measures, developers can significantly reduce the risk of injection attacks, XSS, and other security breaches. Combining manual code reviews, proper error handling, and the use of automated tools further enhances the security posture of applications.

2.2 Output Encoding and Data Validation

Output encoding and data validation are essential security practices that help prevent vulnerabilities like cross-site scripting (XSS) and data manipulation attacks. This section explores the importance of output encoding and data validation, their role in ensuring secure application output, and best practices for their implementation.

2.2.1 Importance of Output Encoding

Output encoding is the process of converting special characters and symbols into their corresponding HTML entities or other safe representations. It ensures that user-supplied or dynamically generated content is treated as data rather than executable code by the browser.

Output encoding plays a critical role in preventing cross-site scripting (XSS) attacks. By encoding output, developers can neutralize any malicious script or code injected by attackers, preventing it from being executed and protecting users from potential harm.

2.2.2 Common Output Encoding Techniques

There are several techniques and libraries available for implementing output encoding effectively. Here are some commonly used approaches:

HTML Entity Encoding: Convert special characters to their respective HTML entities, such as < for < and > for >. This prevents the browser from interpreting the characters as part of the HTML structure.

Contextual Encoding: Apply encoding based on the specific context in which the output is being used. For example, different encoding may be required for attribute values, text content, or URL parameters.

Output Encoding Libraries: Many programming languages and frameworks provide built-in functions or libraries for output encoding. Utilize these libraries to simplify the encoding process and ensure consistent and secure output.

2.2.3 Importance of Data Validation

Data validation is the process of verifying that data meets specific criteria or constraints. It ensures that data used within an application is valid, reliable, and consistent. By implementing data validation, developers can detect and handle invalid or unexpected data, preventing potential security issues.

Data validation is essential for maintaining data integrity and preventing data manipulation attacks. It helps protect against input that may exploit vulnerabilities, compromise system functionality, or cause unintended consequences.

2.2.4 Common Data Validation Techniques

To effectively validate data, developers should consider the following techniques:

Format Validation: Verify that data adheres to the expected format, such as email addresses, phone numbers, or social security numbers. Regular expressions or built-in language functions can be used to perform format validation.

Range and Boundary Validation: Ensure that numeric or date data falls within the expected range or boundaries. For example, check that a user's age is within a reasonable range or that a date falls within specific limits.

Length and Size Validation: Validate the length or size of data to ensure it is within acceptable limits. This helps prevent buffer overflows, denial-of-service attacks, and other vulnerabilities caused by excessive input.

Whitelisting and Blacklisting: Use whitelist or blacklist approaches to validate and filter data. Whitelisting allows only predefined, trusted values, while blacklisting blocks known malicious or invalid values. Whitelisting is generally more secure, as it explicitly defines what is allowed rather than trying to account for all possible malicious inputs.

2.2.5 Validation and Sanitization of User-Generated Content

User-generated content, such as comments, forum posts, or user profiles, often requires special attention in terms of validation and sanitization. It is crucial to validate and sanitize user-generated content to prevent XSS attacks and ensure the integrity of the overall application.

Validate user-generated content to enforce constraints on the allowed input, such as character limits or disallowed HTML tags. Additionally, sanitize the content by applying appropriate output encoding techniques to neutralize any potential malicious code.

2.2.6 Secure Handling of Error Messages and Debug Information

When handling error messages and debug information, it is important to follow secure coding practices. Avoid exposing sensitive information, stack traces, or system details in error messages that could aid attackers in understanding the application's vulnerabilities.

Error messages should provide minimal information to users while still being helpful for troubleshooting. Log and handle errors securely, ensuring that sensitive information is not leaked in logs or error reports.

2.2.7 The Role of Automated Tools

Automated security scanners and code analysis tools can assist in identifying output encoding and data validation issues in codebases. These tools can help detect potential vulnerabilities and suggest improvements, but they should not be solely relied upon. Manual code reviews and thorough testing are crucial for a comprehensive security assessment.

In conclusion, output encoding and data validation are vital practices for ensuring the security and integrity of application output. By implementing effective output encoding techniques, developers can mitigate the risk of XSS attacks and protect users from malicious code execution. Additionally, data validation helps maintain data integrity and prevents data manipulation attacks. Leveraging automated tools, following secure coding practices, and conducting regular security assessments contribute to building robust and secure applications.

2.3 Error Handling and Logging

Proper error handling and logging are critical aspects of secure coding. They help developers identify and respond to errors, debug issues, and maintain the security and stability of the application. This section explores the importance of error handling and logging, best practices for implementing them securely, and their role in enhancing the overall security of the system.

2.3.1 Importance of Error Handling

Error handling is the process of detecting, reporting, and responding to errors that occur during the execution of an application. Effective error handling is crucial for maintaining the reliability and security of the system. It allows developers to identify and address errors promptly, reducing the risk of security vulnerabilities and improving the user experience.

Proper error handling prevents information leakage that could aid attackers in understanding the system's inner workings. It ensures that error messages do not disclose sensitive information, such as database credentials, system paths, or stack traces, which could be exploited by malicious actors.

2.3.2 Secure Error Handling Practices

To implement secure error handling, consider the following best practices:

Use Generic Error Messages: Avoid displaying detailed error messages to end-users, as this could provide valuable information to attackers. Instead, provide user-friendly and generic error messages that do not reveal specific details about the underlying issue.

Log Errors Securely: Log errors for diagnostic and troubleshooting purposes, but ensure that sensitive information is not included in the logs. Avoid logging sensitive data, user credentials, or any other personally identifiable information (PII). Implement proper access controls and encryption for log files to protect them from unauthorized access.

Handle Errors Gracefully: Design error handling routines to handle exceptions and errors gracefully. Displaying a custom error page or a friendly message to the user can enhance the user experience and mitigate the risk of exposing system details.

Avoid Excessive Error Detail: When displaying error messages during development or debugging, be cautious not to reveal excessive error details. Developers should have access to detailed error information, but ensure that it is not exposed in production environments.

Validate and Sanitize Error Input: When displaying error messages that include user input, ensure that the input is properly validated and sanitized to prevent XSS attacks or injection of malicious code.

2.3.3 Importance of Logging

Logging is the process of recording events and activities within an application or system. It is a crucial aspect of security monitoring, auditing, and troubleshooting. Proper logging allows developers and administrators to track and analyze the behavior of the application, detect anomalies, and identify potential security breaches.

Logging security-relevant events, such as login attempts, privilege changes, or access control failures, provides a valuable source of information for incident response and forensic analysis. It enables the identification of suspicious activities and aids in understanding the scope and impact of security incidents.

2.3.4 Secure Logging Practices

To implement secure logging, consider the following best practices:

Log Security-Relevant Events: Focus on logging events that are relevant to the security of the application, such as authentication and authorization events, access control violations, and critical system operations.

Minimize Sensitive Data in Logs: Avoid logging sensitive information, including user credentials, credit card numbers, or other PII. If necessary, obfuscate or redact sensitive information to protect user privacy.

Implement Log Integrity and Confidentiality: Ensure that log files are protected from unauthorized modifications and access. Apply appropriate access controls and encryption to maintain the integrity and confidentiality of log data.

Log Sufficient Contextual Information: Include relevant contextual information in log entries to facilitate troubleshooting and incident response. This may include timestamps, user identifiers, session IDs, and details of the request or operation being performed.

Regularly Monitor and Analyze Logs: Regularly review and analyze logs to identify any suspicious activities or signs of potential security breaches.

Implement automated log monitoring and alerting systems to detect anomalies or patterns indicative of security incidents.

2.3.5 Error Handling and Logging in Production

When deploying applications to production environments, it is crucial to ensure that error handling and logging mechanisms are properly configured and optimized. Consider the following practices:

Disable Detailed Error Messages: Disable detailed error messages in production environments to prevent the exposure of sensitive information to potential attackers. Instead, log detailed error information for later analysis and debugging purposes.

Implement Centralized Logging: Use a centralized logging system to aggregate and analyze logs from different application components or server instances. This allows for centralized monitoring, analysis, and correlation of log data, simplifying security incident detection and response.

Implement Log Retention and Backup Strategies: Define log retention policies and implement regular log backups. This ensures that log data is retained for an appropriate duration to meet compliance requirements and enables analysis of historical logs for forensic purposes.

Regularly Review Logs: Schedule regular log reviews and analysis to proactively identify security incidents, performance issues, or other anomalies. Actively monitor logs for signs of suspicious activities and promptly respond to any identified issues.

In conclusion, error handling and logging are essential components of secure coding practices. Proper error handling prevents information leakage and enhances the user experience, while secure logging enables monitoring, analysis, and detection of security incidents. By following best practices and implementing robust error handling and logging mechanisms, developers can improve the security and reliability of their applications.

2.4 Secure Configuration Management

Secure configuration management is a crucial aspect of developing and deploying secure applications. It involves managing and maintaining the configuration settings and options of software components, frameworks, servers, and other elements of the application ecosystem. This section explores the importance of secure configuration management, best practices for its implementation, and its role in mitigating security risks.

2.4.1 Importance of Secure Configuration Management

Secure configuration management helps ensure that software components and systems are properly configured to mitigate potential security risks. Inadequate configuration settings can expose vulnerabilities and create opportunities for attackers to exploit the application or system.

Proper configuration management reduces the attack surface and strengthens the overall security posture of the application. It involves implementing secure defaults, disabling unnecessary features or services, applying appropriate access controls, and regularly updating and patching software components.

2.4.2 Secure Configuration Management Best Practices

To implement secure configuration management, consider the following best practices:

Implement Secure Defaults: Set secure default configurations for software components and systems. This includes enabling security features, disabling unnecessary services, and applying secure communication protocols by default.

Harden Servers and Systems: Securely configure servers and systems by following established hardening guidelines. This involves disabling unnecessary ports, services, or protocols, configuring strong authentication mechanisms, and applying access controls based on the principle of least privilege.

Regularly Update and Patch Components: Keep software components, frameworks, and libraries up to date by regularly applying security patches and updates. Establish a process for monitoring and promptly responding to security advisories and vulnerability disclosures.

Secure Database and Storage Configurations: Configure databases and storage systems securely by applying access controls, encrypting sensitive data, and implementing secure connection protocols. Use strong and unique credentials for database access and enforce secure password policies.

Secure Network Configuration: Implement secure network configurations by segmenting networks, using firewalls to control traffic flow, and applying secure communication protocols such as HTTPS. Disable or restrict unnecessary network services to minimize the attack surface.

Restrict Administrative Access: Limit administrative access to critical components and systems to authorized personnel only. Implement strong authentication mechanisms, such as multi-factor authentication, for administrative accounts and regularly review and update access privileges.

Monitor Configuration Changes: Implement mechanisms to monitor and track changes to configurations. This helps identify unauthorized modifications or configuration drift that could introduce security vulnerabilities. Regularly review and audit configuration settings to ensure compliance with security requirements.

2.4.3 Secure Development Environments

In addition to securing the production environment, it is crucial to maintain secure development environments. Secure development environments should mirror the production environment as closely as possible, including configuration settings, security controls, and access privileges.

Developers should adhere to secure coding practices in the development environment, apply secure configuration settings for development tools and frameworks, and ensure that test data does not contain sensitive information. Regularly review and update development environment configurations to align with the latest security best practices.

2.4.4 Configuration Management in Deployment Pipelines

Secure configuration management should be integrated into the deployment pipelines and continuous integration/continuous deployment (CI/CD) processes. This ensures that secure configurations are applied consistently throughout the development, testing, and deployment phases.

Automate the configuration management process where possible, using configuration management tools or infrastructure-as-code approaches. This helps enforce consistent and repeatable configurations and reduces the risk of human errors or deviations from secure configurations.

2.4.5 Regular Configuration Audits

Regular configuration audits are essential to validate and maintain the security of the application ecosystem. Conduct periodic audits to review configuration settings, identify misconfigurations, and ensure compliance with security standards and industry best practices.

Perform vulnerability scanning and configuration assessment to detect any deviations from secure configurations. Use configuration management tools or specialized security tools to automate and streamline the configuration auditing process.

In conclusion, secure configuration management is crucial for mitigating security risks and maintaining a robust security posture for applications and systems. By implementing secure defaults, regularly updating configurations, and adhering to best practices, developers can reduce the attack surface and protect against potential vulnerabilities. Secure configuration management should be an integral part of the development lifecycle, from development environments to production deployments.

2.5 Secure Coding Standards and Frameworks

Secure coding standards and frameworks provide guidelines, best practices, and predefined secure coding patterns to help developers write secure code. They promote consistent coding practices, address common security vulnerabilities, and enhance the overall security of applications. This section explores the importance of secure coding standards and frameworks, their benefits, and how to effectively incorporate them into the development process.

2.5.1 Importance of Secure Coding Standards

Secure coding standards play a vital role in ensuring the security and reliability of software applications.

They provide developers with a set of rules and guidelines for writing secure code, focusing on areas such as input validation, output encoding, authentication, access control, and error handling. By adhering to secure coding standards, developers can reduce the risk of introducing security vulnerabilities into their codebase.

Secure coding standards also promote consistency and maintainability in code development. They help teams collaborate effectively, improve code readability, and facilitate code reviews and audits. Furthermore, adhering to established standards ensures that security is considered from the early stages of development, making it easier to implement security controls and identify potential vulnerabilities.

2.5.2 Benefits of Secure Coding Frameworks

Secure coding frameworks offer pre-defined libraries, modules, and components that developers can leverage to build secure applications. These frameworks encapsulate security best practices and provide ready-to-use functionality, reducing the complexity and effort required to implement security measures from scratch.

The benefits of using secure coding frameworks include:

Built-in Security Controls: Secure coding frameworks incorporate security controls, such as input validation, output encoding, access control, and encryption, into their core functionality. This reduces the likelihood of security vulnerabilities and makes it easier for developers to follow secure coding practices.

Reduced Development Time: By leveraging secure coding frameworks, developers can save time and effort by utilizing pre-tested and validated security components. This allows them to focus on application-specific logic rather than reinventing security measures.

Community Support and Updates: Secure coding frameworks often have active developer communities that contribute to their improvement, provide support, and share knowledge and best practices. Regular updates and security patches ensure that the frameworks stay current with emerging threats and vulnerabilities.

Compliance and Audit Readiness: Using established secure coding frameworks can help organizations demonstrate compliance with security standards and regulations. Frameworks that align with industry-recognized standards, such as OWASP (Open Web Application Security Project) or CERT (Computer Emergency Response Team), provide a solid foundation for security audits and assessments.

2.5.3 Incorporating Secure Coding Standards and Frameworks

To effectively incorporate secure coding standards and frameworks into the development process, consider the following steps:

Select Appropriate Standards and Frameworks: Evaluate and choose secure coding standards and frameworks that align with your application's requirements, technology stack, and industry best practices. Consider frameworks that have a strong community, regular updates, and good documentation.

Establish Development Guidelines: Create coding guidelines based on the selected secure coding standards. These guidelines should address common security vulnerabilities and provide specific recommendations for different coding scenarios. Make the guidelines easily accessible to all developers and provide training and education on their proper implementation.

Conduct Secure Code Reviews: Integrate secure code reviews as part of your development process. Assign experienced developers or security specialists to review code for adherence to secure coding standards, identify vulnerabilities, and provide feedback and recommendations for improvement.

Provide Developer Training: Offer training programs and workshops to educate developers on secure coding practices and the proper use of secure coding frameworks. This will enhance their understanding of security principles and enable them to effectively utilize the provided frameworks.

Automated Code Analysis: Utilize automated code analysis tools that can scan codebases for security vulnerabilities, adherence to coding standards, and best practices. These tools can provide instant feedback to developers, flag potential issues, and enforce compliance with secure coding standards.

Continuously Update Standards and Frameworks: Regularly review and update your chosen secure coding standards and frameworks to ensure they align with the latest security practices and emerging threats. Stay informed about new vulnerabilities and evolving security risks to adapt your standards and frameworks accordingly.

By integrating secure coding standards and leveraging secure coding frameworks, developers can enhance the security of their applications, reduce vulnerabilities, and maintain a consistent approach to secure coding practices. This not only strengthens the resilience of the application but also contributes to building a security-conscious development culture within the organization.

Chapter 3: Threat Modeling and Risk Assessment

Welcome to Chapter 3 of "The Secure Coder's Handbook: A Practical Guide to Secure Development." In this chapter, we explore the critical concepts of threat modeling and risk assessment. By understanding potential threats and assessing their risks, we can prioritize our efforts and effectively mitigate security vulnerabilities.

Threat modeling is a proactive approach that helps us identify and analyze potential threats to our applications and systems. By systematically analyzing the security posture of our software, we can anticipate potential attacks and vulnerabilities. In this chapter, we will discuss different threat modeling methodologies, such as STRIDE (Spoofing, Tampering, Repudiation, Information disclosure, Denial of service, Elevation of privilege), and explore how to apply them effectively. We will also delve into the process of identifying and prioritizing potential threats, considering both technical and business impacts.

Risk assessment is the process of evaluating the likelihood and impact of identified threats. It allows us to quantify and prioritize risks, enabling us to allocate our resources effectively. In this chapter, we will discuss various risk assessment techniques, such as qualitative and quantitative risk assessment, and examine how to assess the potential impact of threats on our applications and systems. By understanding the potential risks, we can make informed decisions about security controls and mitigation strategies.

We will also explore the importance of security code reviews and audits as part of the threat modeling and risk assessment process. Conducting regular code reviews helps identify vulnerabilities and security weaknesses early in the development lifecycle. We will discuss techniques for conducting effective code reviews and explore the role of automated tools in supporting this process. Additionally, we will delve into the significance of security audits, both internal and external, and how they can help uncover hidden vulnerabilities.

Throughout this chapter, we emphasize the need for collaboration and communication when performing threat modeling and risk assessment. By involving various stakeholders, including developers, architects, security professionals, and business owners, we can gather diverse perspectives and insights, ensuring a comprehensive assessment of potential threats and risks. We will discuss effective communication strategies to facilitate productive discussions and decision-making processes.

Furthermore, we will explore the iterative nature of threat modeling and risk assessment. Security threats evolve over time, and new vulnerabilities emerge. Therefore, it is crucial to regularly revisit and update our threat models and risk assessments to adapt to changing circumstances. We will discuss how to incorporate threat modeling and risk assessment into our development workflows, making them an integral part of the software development lifecycle.

In conclusion, Chapter 3 equips us with the knowledge and tools to perform effective threat modeling and risk assessment. By identifying potential threats, quantifying risks, and involving stakeholders in the process, we can prioritize our efforts and allocate resources to mitigate security vulnerabilities effectively. Threat modeling and risk assessment provide a proactive approach to secure development, ensuring that our applications and systems are resilient against potential attacks.

In the subsequent chapters, we will continue our exploration of secure development practices, including secure authentication and authorization mechanisms, securing data storage and transmission, securing web applications, and developing secure mobile and IoT applications. By combining the principles and practices learned in previous chapters with the insights gained from threat modeling and risk assessment, we will build robust and secure software applications.

So, let's dive into the world of threat modeling and risk assessment. By embracing these practices, we can better understand potential security risks and make informed decisions to protect our applications and systems.

3.1 Understanding the Threat Modeling Process

Threat modeling is a systematic approach to identifying, assessing, and mitigating potential threats and vulnerabilities in software applications. It helps developers and security professionals proactively analyze and understand the security risks associated with an application, allowing for the implementation of effective security controls. This section explores the importance of threat modeling, the key steps involved in the process, and the benefits it provides to secure development.

3.1.1 Importance of Threat Modeling

Threat modeling is a critical activity in the secure development lifecycle. It enables developers to anticipate potential threats and vulnerabilities early in the design phase, rather than reacting to them after deployment. By understanding the application's attack surface, weaknesses, and potential exploit scenarios, developers can make informed decisions and prioritize security measures.

The benefits of threat modeling include:

Proactive Risk Mitigation: Threat modeling helps identify and prioritize potential threats and vulnerabilities before they can be exploited. By addressing these risks early in the development process, developers can implement appropriate security controls and mitigate the impact of potential attacks.

Cost-Efficiency: Addressing security vulnerabilities in the design phase is more cost-effective than fixing them at later stages of development or after deployment. Threat modeling allows for early detection and resolution of security issues, reducing the likelihood of costly security breaches and subsequent remediation efforts.

Alignment with Business Objectives: Threat modeling helps align security measures with business objectives and requirements. By understanding the potential threats and their impact on the organization, developers can tailor security controls to protect critical assets and ensure business continuity.

Enhanced Collaboration: Threat modeling encourages collaboration between development teams, security professionals, and stakeholders. By involving multiple perspectives, diverse expertise, and shared knowledge, the threat modeling process facilitates a comprehensive understanding of the application's security risks and promotes effective risk mitigation strategies.

3.1.2 Key Steps in the Threat Modeling Process

The threat modeling process typically involves the following steps:

Define the System: Start by clearly defining the scope of the system being analyzed. Identify its components, interfaces, dependencies, and the data flows between them. This step helps establish a comprehensive understanding of the application's architecture.

Identify Threats: Identify potential threats and attack vectors that the application may be exposed to. Consider both technical threats, such as injection attacks or privilege escalation, and non-technical threats, such as social engineering or physical attacks.

Assess Vulnerabilities: Analyze the system's architecture, design, and implementation to identify vulnerabilities that could be exploited by the identified threats. This includes reviewing code, configurations, third-party dependencies, and system interactions.

Determine Risks: Evaluate the potential impact and likelihood of each identified threat. Assess the risks associated with the vulnerabilities, considering factors such as the value of the compromised assets, potential damage, and the likelihood of successful exploitation.

Prioritize and Mitigate: Prioritize the identified risks based on their severity and potential impact. Develop strategies to mitigate each risk, considering appropriate security controls, countermeasures, and best practices. This may include code changes, architectural improvements, or the implementation of security frameworks.

Validate and Iterate: Validate the effectiveness of the implemented security measures through testing and validation. Continuously review and update the threat model as new information or changes to the system arise. The threat modeling process should be iterative, adapting to evolving threats and system changes.

3.1.3 Tools and Techniques for Threat Modeling

Several tools and techniques can aid in the threat modeling process, including:

Data Flow Diagrams (DFDs): DFDs help visualize the flow of data within the application and identify potential points of vulnerability or data exposure.

Attack Trees: Attack trees provide a structured representation of potential attack paths, starting from high-level objectives and branching into more specific attack scenarios.

STRIDE Model: The STRIDE model (Spoofing, Tampering, Repudiation, Information Disclosure, Denial of Service, Elevation of Privilege) is a framework that helps identify common threat categories and their associated risks.

Threat Modeling Tools: Various commercial and open-source threat modeling tools are available to assist in the process. These tools often provide templates, libraries of threats and vulnerabilities, and automation capabilities to streamline the threat modeling workflow.

By following the threat modeling process and utilizing appropriate tools and techniques, developers can systematically identify and address security risks, resulting in more robust and resilient applications. Threat modeling should be an integral part of the secure development lifecycle, enabling proactive security measures and reinforcing a security-conscious mindset within the development team.

3.2 Identifying and Prioritizing Security Risks

Identifying and prioritizing security risks is a crucial step in the threat modeling and risk assessment process. It involves systematically analyzing the potential threats and vulnerabilities associated with an application and determining their level of risk based on factors such as impact and likelihood. This section explores the methods and techniques for identifying and prioritizing security risks effectively.

3.2.1 Methods for Identifying Security Risks

To identify security risks, consider the following methods:

Threat Brainstorming: Conduct brainstorming sessions with stakeholders, developers, and security professionals to identify potential threats and vulnerabilities. Encourage open discussion and capture as many potential risks as possible.

Security Standards and Guidelines: Refer to established security standards, guidelines, and best practices specific to the application's domain or technology stack. These resources often highlight common security risks and provide recommendations for mitigation.

Security Testing and Assessments: Perform security testing activities such as penetration testing, vulnerability scanning, and code reviews to identify potential security vulnerabilities. These assessments help uncover weaknesses that could be exploited by attackers.

Knowledge Sharing and Experience: Leverage the collective knowledge and experience of the development team and security experts. Encourage sharing of past incidents, lessons learned, and industry-specific security concerns to identify risks specific to the application.

Threat Libraries and Databases: Refer to threat libraries, databases, and repositories such as the Common Weakness Enumeration (CWE) or the Open Web Application Security Project (OWASP) Top Ten. These resources catalog common vulnerabilities and associated risks, providing valuable insights for risk identification.

3.2.2 Factors for Prioritizing Security Risks

Once the security risks are identified, it is essential to prioritize them to allocate appropriate resources and address the most critical risks first. Consider the following factors when prioritizing security risks:

Impact: Assess the potential impact of a security risk on the application, system, or organization. Consider factors such as data confidentiality, integrity, availability, regulatory compliance, financial loss, reputational damage, and potential harm to users.

Likelihood: Evaluate the likelihood of a security risk being exploited or occurring. Consider factors such as the ease of exploitation, historical data or incidents, known attack vectors, and the application's exposure to potential attackers.

Attack Surface: Analyze the surface area of the application that is exposed to potential threats. Assess the number of entry points, interfaces, integrations, and components that could be targeted by attackers. A larger attack surface increases the likelihood of security risks.

Vulnerability Severity: Consider the severity of the vulnerabilities associated with each identified risk. Evaluate the ease of exploitation, potential impact, and the existence of known exploits or proof-of-concept demonstrations.

Business Impact: Assess the potential business impact of a security risk. Consider the criticality of the affected assets or functions, the organization's reliance on the application, and the potential disruption to business operations or customer trust.

Time and Resources: Evaluate the feasibility of addressing the security risk within the given time frame and resource constraints. Consider the effort required to implement necessary security controls and the availability of resources, expertise, and budget.

By considering these factors, you can prioritize security risks effectively and focus on mitigating the most critical and high-risk vulnerabilities. The prioritization process helps allocate resources efficiently, reduce the overall risk exposure, and ensure that security efforts align with the business objectives and risk tolerance of the organization.

Remember that prioritization should be an ongoing process, as new risks may emerge, and the risk landscape can change over time. Regular reviews and updates to the risk assessment are necessary to adapt to evolving threats and to address emerging risks effectively.

3.3 Mitigating Risks through Secure Design Principles

Mitigating security risks through secure design principles is a fundamental aspect of the threat modeling and risk assessment process. Secure design principles guide the development of applications with security in mind, ensuring that robust security controls are integrated into the application's architecture and functionality. This section explores key secure design principles and their application in risk mitigation.

3.3.1 Principle of Least Privilege

The principle of least privilege states that users and processes should be granted only the minimum privileges necessary to perform their required tasks. By implementing this principle, you can reduce the potential impact of a security breach or unauthorized access. When designing an application, consider the following:

User Roles and Access Controls: Define different user roles based on their responsibilities and restrict access privileges accordingly. Implement access controls to ensure that users can only perform actions that are necessary for their roles.

Privilege Separation: Separate different components or modules of the application and assign appropriate privileges to each component. Limit access to sensitive resources and functionality to authorized components only.

Default Deny: Design the application with a default deny mindset, meaning that access to resources or functionality should be explicitly granted, rather than relying on implicit permissions. This approach helps prevent unintended access or privilege escalation.

3.3.2 Defense in Depth

The defense in depth principle involves implementing multiple layers of security controls to protect against potential attacks. Instead of relying on a single security measure, this principle advocates for a layered approach to security. Consider the following:

Perimeter Security: Implement firewalls, intrusion detection systems, and other network-level security measures to protect against external threats.

Application-Level Security: Incorporate security controls within the application, such as input validation, output encoding, and secure authentication and authorization mechanisms.

Data Encryption: Encrypt sensitive data at rest and in transit to protect it from unauthorized access or disclosure. Utilize strong encryption algorithms and follow encryption best practices.

Security Monitoring and Logging: Implement robust logging and monitoring mechanisms to detect and respond to potential security incidents. Regularly review logs and security alerts to identify suspicious activities.

Incident Response and Recovery: Develop an incident response plan that outlines procedures for detecting, responding to, and recovering from security incidents. This ensures a timely and effective response to potential breaches.

3.3.3 Secure Error Handling

Secure error handling is essential for preventing information leakage and minimizing the impact of potential security vulnerabilities. When designing error handling mechanisms, consider the following:

Error Messages: Ensure that error messages do not reveal sensitive information or provide too much information that could be exploited by attackers. Use generic error messages that do not disclose specific details about the system or its vulnerabilities.

Logging and Monitoring: Log errors and exceptions appropriately to aid in troubleshooting and identifying potential security incidents. However, ensure that the logging mechanism does not expose sensitive data or create additional attack vectors.

Graceful Degradation: Design the application to gracefully handle errors and degrade functionality when errors occur. Avoid exposing detailed error information to end-users, which could be leveraged by attackers.

Input Validation and Sanitization: Validate and sanitize user inputs to prevent potential injection attacks and other vulnerabilities. Implement proper input validation techniques, such as white-listing, to ensure that inputs are within acceptable boundaries.

3.3.4 Secure Communication

Secure communication is crucial to protect sensitive data transmitted between components, users, and systems. When designing communication channels, consider the following:

Transport Layer Security (TLS): Utilize TLS protocols to encrypt data in transit, providing confidentiality and integrity. Use the latest TLS versions and strong cipher suites to ensure secure communication.

Secure APIs: Implement secure APIs by utilizing authentication, authorization, and encryption mechanisms. Follow secure coding practices for API development, such as input validation and protection against injection attacks.

Secure Protocols and Standards: Follow industry best practices and security standards for communication protocols, such as HTTPS for web applications, SSH for secure remote access, and SFTP for secure file transfers.

Data Validation: Validate and sanitize data received from external sources or transmitted over communication channels to prevent potential attacks such as command injection or SQL injection.

By incorporating these secure design principles into the application architecture and development process, you can significantly reduce the potential for security vulnerabilities and enhance the overall security posture of the application. Secure design principles should be considered from the early stages of development and consistently applied throughout the software development lifecycle to ensure a robust and secure application.

3.4 Conducting Security Code Reviews and Audits

Security code reviews and audits are essential activities in ensuring the robustness and resilience of an application's codebase. They involve systematically examining the application's source code to identify security vulnerabilities, coding errors, and adherence to secure coding practices. This section explores the importance of conducting security code reviews and audits and provides guidelines for their effective execution.

3.4.1 Importance of Security Code Reviews and Audits

Security code reviews and audits play a crucial role in identifying and addressing security vulnerabilities in the application's codebase. They provide the following benefits:

Vulnerability Identification: Code reviews and audits help identify potential security vulnerabilities, such as input validation flaws, insecure coding patterns, access control issues, or cryptographic weaknesses. Detecting these vulnerabilities early allows for prompt remediation, reducing the likelihood of exploitation.

Compliance and Best Practice Adherence: Security code reviews and audits ensure compliance with relevant security standards, guidelines, and regulations. They help confirm adherence to secure coding practices, industry-specific requirements, and organizational policies.

Quality Assurance: By reviewing and auditing the code, developers can identify coding errors, logic flaws, and performance issues that may impact the application's security and overall quality. Addressing these issues enhances the reliability and stability of the application.

Knowledge Sharing and Skill Development: Code reviews and audits facilitate knowledge sharing among team members. They provide an opportunity for developers to learn from each other, exchange best practices, and enhance their understanding of secure coding principles and techniques.

3.4.2 Guidelines for Conducting Security Code Reviews and Audits

To ensure effective and comprehensive security code reviews and audits, consider the following guidelines:

Establish Review Criteria: Define clear criteria for the code review and audit process. This may include specific security requirements, coding standards, and best practices that the code must adhere to. Provide guidelines or checklists to guide reviewers in identifying potential security issues.

Involve Multiple Reviewers: Engage multiple reviewers with diverse expertise, including developers, security professionals, and subject matter experts. The involvement of different perspectives helps identify a broader range of security vulnerabilities and promotes comprehensive analysis.

Use Static Analysis Tools: Employ automated static analysis tools to assist in the code review process. These tools can detect common security vulnerabilities, coding errors, and adherence to coding standards. However, remember that manual review is still essential to uncover more complex or context-specific vulnerabilities.

Review Security Controls: Assess the implementation of security controls, such as authentication, authorization, input validation, output encoding, and secure communication. Verify that these controls are properly implemented, correctly invoked, and effectively mitigate the associated security risks.

Validate Cryptographic Implementations: If the application involves cryptographic operations, carefully review and validate their implementation. Ensure that encryption algorithms, key management, and cryptographic protocols adhere to industry best practices and recommended standards.

Analyze Error Handling and Logging: Evaluate how the application handles errors, exceptions, and logging. Verify that error messages do not disclose sensitive information, log entries are appropriately protected, and potential security incidents are appropriately logged for analysis.

Test for Security Scenarios: Consider conducting security-focused testing during the code review and audit process. This may include testing for common vulnerabilities, such as injection attacks, cross-site scripting (XSS), cross-site request forgery (CSRF), and other security-related scenarios.

Document Findings and Remediation Steps: Document the identified security issues, vulnerabilities, and recommendations for remediation. Provide clear explanations of the risks associated with each finding and provide guidance on how to address them effectively.

Follow Up and Track Remediation: Track the progress of addressing identified security issues and ensure that remediation actions are implemented. Regularly communicate with the development team to address any questions or clarifications regarding the findings.

By following these guidelines, organizations can conduct thorough and effective security code reviews and audits, leading to the identification and mitigation of security vulnerabilities. These activities contribute significantly to building secure and robust applications, reducing the risk of successful attacks and ensuring the protection of critical assets and user data.

Chapter 4: Secure Authentication and Authorization

Welcome to Chapter 4 of "The Secure Coder's Handbook: A Practical Guide to Secure Development." In this chapter, we delve into the crucial topics of secure authentication and authorization. By implementing robust authentication and authorization mechanisms, we can ensure that only authorized individuals can access sensitive resources within our applications.

Authentication is the process of verifying the identity of a user or entity. It is the foundation of secure access control and protects against unauthorized access. In this chapter, we explore various authentication techniques, including password-based authentication, multi-factor authentication (MFA), biometrics, and token-based authentication. We discuss the strengths and weaknesses of each approach and provide guidance on selecting the most appropriate authentication mechanism based on the requirements of our applications.

Authorization, on the other hand, determines what actions a user or entity is allowed to perform within an application or system. It ensures that users have the necessary privileges to access and manipulate resources securely. In this chapter, we delve into different authorization models, such as role-based access control (RBAC) and attribute-based access control (ABAC). We discuss the benefits and considerations of each model and provide practical examples of how to implement granular and secure authorization mechanisms.

We also examine the importance of secure session management in the context of authentication and authorization. Sessions play a vital role in maintaining user state and managing user interactions. However, if not implemented securely, they can become a target for attacks such as session hijacking and session fixation. We discuss techniques for secure session management, including session token generation, expiration, and protection against session-related vulnerabilities.

Furthermore, we explore secure password storage and management. Passwords are the most common form of user authentication, and their proper handling is crucial to ensure the security of user accounts. We discuss password hashing algorithms, salting, and techniques for securely storing and managing passwords. Additionally, we address common password-related vulnerabilities, such as weak passwords and password reuse, and provide guidance on enforcing strong password policies.

In the context of web applications, we explore the significance of protecting against common authentication and authorization vulnerabilities, including brute force attacks, session hijacking, and privilege escalation. We discuss preventive measures, such as account lockouts, session expiration, and least privilege principles, to mitigate these vulnerabilities effectively.

Throughout this chapter, we emphasize the importance of secure authentication and authorization as fundamental components of secure coding practices. By implementing robust authentication mechanisms, enforcing strong password policies, implementing secure session management, and employing granular authorization models, we can protect our applications and users from unauthorized access and potential security breaches.

In the subsequent chapters, we will continue to explore specific aspects of secure development, including securing data storage and transmission, securing web applications, developing secure mobile and IoT applications, and addressing common vulnerabilities. By combining the principles and practices learned in previous chapters with the insights gained from secure authentication and authorization, we will build software applications that are more resilient and less susceptible to unauthorized access.

So, let's delve into the world of secure authentication and authorization. By embracing these techniques, we can ensure that only authorized individuals have access to our applications and resources, safeguarding the confidentiality and integrity of our systems.

4.1 Authentication Mechanisms: Usernames, Passwords, and Beyond

Authentication is a critical aspect of secure development, as it verifies the identities of users and ensures that only authorized individuals can access sensitive resources or perform specific actions. This section focuses on authentication mechanisms, including traditional username-password authentication and explores advanced authentication techniques for enhanced security.

4.1.1 Traditional Username-Password Authentication

Username-password authentication is a widely used mechanism for verifying user identities. It involves the following components:

Usernames: Usernames provide unique identifiers for individual users within the system. They should be unique, easily identifiable, and should not expose sensitive information.

Passwords: Passwords serve as secret credentials known only to the user. To ensure password security, consider the following best practices:

Password Complexity: Enforce the use of strong passwords that include a combination of uppercase and lowercase letters, numbers, and special characters. Encourage users to create passwords that are not easily guessable or dictionary-based.

Password Hashing: Store passwords securely by applying strong cryptographic hash functions, such as bcrypt or Argon2, to prevent their direct retrieval. Hashing adds an additional layer of protection by converting passwords into irreversible values.

Password Policies: Implement password policies that define minimum length, expiration periods, and restrictions on password reuse to promote better password hygiene.

Multi-Factor Authentication (MFA): Consider implementing MFA, which combines two or more authentication factors (e.g., password, fingerprint, SMS code) to enhance security. MFA adds an extra layer of protection by requiring users to provide additional evidence of their identity.

4.1.2 Advanced Authentication Techniques

Beyond traditional username-password authentication, there are several advanced authentication techniques that can provide stronger security measures:

Biometric Authentication: Biometric authentication uses unique physical or behavioral characteristics, such as fingerprints, facial recognition, or iris scans, to verify user identities. Biometrics offer a high level of security but require appropriate hardware and software support.

Token-Based Authentication: Token-based authentication involves the use of security tokens, such as smart cards, hardware tokens, or mobile authentication apps. These tokens generate time-based or event-based codes that users must provide along with their usernames and passwords for authentication.

Single Sign-On (SSO): SSO enables users to authenticate once and gain access to multiple applications or systems without requiring repeated login credentials. SSO centralized authentication and simplifies the user experience, reducing the risk of weak or reused passwords.

Social Login: Social login allows users to authenticate using their social media accounts (e.g.,

Facebook, Google). It simplifies the registration and login process, but organizations must ensure the secure handling of user data and the integration with trusted identity providers.

Adaptive Authentication: Adaptive authentication employs risk-based analysis and context-aware factors to dynamically assess the security level required for authentication. It considers factors such as user behavior, location, and device characteristics to determine the appropriate level of authentication for each user interaction.

Passwordless Authentication: Passwordless authentication eliminates the need for traditional passwords and replaces them with alternative authentication factors. Examples include email-based verification codes, biometrics, hardware tokens, or public-key cryptography.

When implementing authentication mechanisms, consider factors such as user experience, scalability, and the specific security requirements of the application. It is crucial to balance security with usability to ensure a seamless and secure authentication process for users.

Remember that authentication is just the first step in access control. Authorization mechanisms, which determine what actions users can perform within the system, are equally important for securing sensitive resources and maintaining data confidentiality and integrity. The combination of strong authentication and authorization mechanisms forms the foundation of a robust and secure access control system.

4.2 Multi-Factor Authentication and Biometrics

Multi-Factor Authentication (MFA) and biometric authentication are advanced security measures that provide enhanced protection against unauthorized access and credential theft. This section explores the concepts and benefits of MFA and biometrics in secure authentication.

4.2.1 Multi-Factor Authentication (MFA)

Multi-Factor Authentication (MFA), also known as two-factor authentication (2FA) or multi-step verification, adds an extra layer of security by requiring users to provide multiple authentication factors to prove their identities. MFA combines two or more of the following factors:

Something You Know: This factor involves knowledge-based information that the user possesses, such as a password, a personal identification number (PIN), or answers to security questions.

Something You Have: This factor relies on possession of a physical object, such as a security token, a smart card, or a mobile device.

Something You Are: This factor is based on a user's unique physical or behavioral characteristics, known as biometric factors. Biometric authentication verifies identities using features such as fingerprints, facial recognition, iris scans, or voice recognition.

The use of multiple factors significantly strengthens authentication security. Even if one factor is compromised, an attacker would still need to bypass additional authentication measures to gain unauthorized access. MFA reduces the risk of unauthorized access due to weak or stolen passwords and provides an additional layer of protection against various attack vectors, such as phishing, brute force attacks, and credential stuffing.

Organizations should consider implementing MFA for sensitive systems, administrative privileges, or any scenario where an extra layer of security is required. MFA can be implemented using various methods, such as One-Time Password (OTP) tokens, SMS or email verification codes, mobile authentication apps, or hardware tokens. The choice of MFA method depends on factors such as cost, usability, and the specific security requirements of the application or system.

4.2.2 Biometric Authentication

Biometric authentication leverages unique physical or behavioral characteristics of individuals to verify their identities. Biometric factors include:

Fingerprint Recognition: This method analyzes the patterns and ridges on a user's fingertip to authenticate their identity.

Facial Recognition: Facial recognition algorithms analyze facial features to verify the user's identity by comparing it with stored templates.

Iris or Retina Scans: These methods use the unique patterns in the iris or retina of the user's eye to authenticate their identity.

Voice Recognition: Voice biometrics analyze the user's vocal characteristics, such as pitch, tone, and speech patterns, to verify their identity.

Biometric authentication offers several advantages:

Strong Security: Biometric factors are unique to individuals and difficult to replicate, providing a high level of security.

User Convenience: Biometric authentication eliminates the need to remember complex passwords or carry physical tokens, enhancing user convenience and usability.

Non-Transferable: Biometric characteristics cannot be easily shared or transferred, reducing the risk of unauthorized access.

However, there are also considerations when implementing biometric authentication:

Privacy and Data Protection: Biometric data is sensitive personal information that requires strict privacy and protection measures. Organizations must adhere to legal and ethical guidelines when collecting, storing, and processing biometric data.

False Positives and False Negatives: Biometric systems may occasionally produce false positive or false negative results, leading to either granting unauthorized access or denying legitimate users. Organizations must carefully evaluate the accuracy and reliability of the chosen biometric system.

Scalability and Compatibility: Implementing biometric authentication may require additional hardware or software components, and compatibility with different devices and platforms should be considered.

When implementing biometric authentication, organizations should carefully evaluate the specific requirements of their applications or systems, user acceptance, privacy concerns, and the availability of reliable biometric technologies.

By incorporating Multi-Factor Authentication and biometric authentication into the authentication mechanisms of an application or system, organizations can significantly enhance the security of user access and reduce the risk of unauthorized access or credential theft. These advanced authentication techniques provide an additional layer of protection, complementing traditional username-password authentication and strengthening overall security.

4.3 Authorization Models: Role-Based, Attribute-Based, and Rule-Based Access Control

Authorization is the process of determining what actions or resources a user can access within an application or system after successful authentication. Different authorization models provide varying levels of granularity and flexibility in managing access control. This section explores three common authorization models: Role-Based Access Control (RBAC), Attribute-Based Access Control (ABAC), and Rule-Based Access Control.

4.3.1 Role-Based Access Control (RBAC)

Role-Based Access Control (RBAC) is a widely adopted authorization model that assigns permissions to users based on their roles within an organization. RBAC simplifies access control management by grouping users into roles and granting permissions to those roles. The key components of RBAC include:

Roles: Roles represent different job functions or responsibilities within the organization. Examples of roles can include "administrator," "manager," or "employee."

Permissions: Permissions define the actions or operations that users with specific roles are allowed to perform. These can include read, write, create, or delete operations on specific resources.

Role-Assignment: Users are assigned one or more roles based on their job function or responsibilities. By associating roles with users, permissions are inherited by the users assigned to those roles.

Role Hierarchy: In some cases, roles can be organized into a hierarchical structure. This allows for the inheritance of permissions from higher-level roles to lower-level roles, simplifying the management of access control.

RBAC provides a flexible and scalable approach to access control, as permissions are defined at the role level, reducing the complexity of managing individual user permissions. RBAC simplifies administration by allowing permissions to be easily assigned or revoked based on changes in user roles or organizational structure.

4.3.2 Attribute-Based Access Control (ABAC)

Attribute-Based Access Control (ABAC) is an authorization model that grants access based on attributes associated with users, resources, and the context of the access request. ABAC considers various attributes, such as user attributes (e.g., department, location), resource attributes (e.g., sensitivity level, classification), and environmental attributes (e.g., time of day, network location) to make access control decisions. The key components of ABAC include:

Policies: Policies define access control rules based on attributes and conditions. These policies specify the allowed or denied access based on the attributes associated with the user, resource, and context.

Attributes: Attributes are characteristics associated with users, resources, or the access request context. These attributes are used to define policies and make access control decisions.

Policy Evaluation: Access control decisions are made by evaluating the policies against the attributes associated with the user, resource, and context.

ABAC provides a more fine-grained and context-aware approach to access control compared to RBAC. It allows for dynamic access control decisions based on specific attributes and conditions, enabling organizations to enforce more precise and flexible access control policies.

4.3.3 Rule-Based Access Control

Rule-Based Access Control (RBAC) is an authorization model that utilizes a set of rules to determine access rights. Rules are defined based on conditions and actions, allowing for more granular control over access. The key components of Rule-Based Access Control include:

Rules: Rules define conditions and actions for access control decisions. Conditions specify the attributes or properties that must be met for the rule to be applied, while actions define the access permissions granted or denied.

Rule Evaluation: Access control decisions are made by evaluating the rules against the conditions and attributes associated with the user, resource, and context.

Rule-Based Access Control offers a flexible and customizable approach to access control by allowing organizations to define specific rules tailored to their requirements. It provides the ability to enforce complex access control policies based on various conditions and actions.

When selecting an authorization model, organizations should consider their specific access control requirements, the complexity of the application or system, and the level of granularity needed for access control. RBAC, ABAC, and Rule-Based Access Control offer different approaches to manage access control and can be combined or customized based on the specific needs of the organization.

By implementing effective authorization models, organizations can ensure that only authorized users have access to the appropriate resources and actions within an application or system. This helps prevent unauthorized access, data breaches, and potential misuse of sensitive information, contributing to overall system security and integrity.

4.4 Securing Session Management and Token-based Authentication

Session management and token-based authentication are essential components of secure authentication and authorization. This section explores best practices for securing session management and implementing token-based authentication to enhance the security of user sessions.

4.4.1 Securing Session Management

Session management is the process of managing user sessions throughout their interaction with an application or system. Sessions allow users to maintain their authenticated state and access authorized resources without repeated authentication for each request. However, inadequate session management can lead to security vulnerabilities, such as session hijacking, session fixation, or session timeout issues. Here are some best practices to secure session management:

Unique Session Identifiers: Each user session should be associated with a unique session identifier. Session identifiers should be long, random, and difficult to predict to prevent session guessing attacks.

Session Expiration and Inactivity Timeout: Define appropriate session expiration and inactivity timeout periods. Sessions should automatically expire after a defined period of inactivity to reduce the risk of unauthorized access due to idle sessions.

Secure Session Storage: Store session identifiers securely, avoiding client-side storage mechanisms vulnerable to client-side attacks. Use server-side storage solutions, such as encrypted cookies or server-based session stores, to store session data securely.

Session Termination: Implement mechanisms to ensure proper session termination. When users log out or perform actions that require session termination, invalidate the associated session identifiers and remove any stored session data.

Session Fixation Protection: Protect against session fixation attacks by generating new session identifiers upon successful authentication and discarding any existing session identifiers.

Transport Layer Security (TLS): Use TLS (formerly SSL) to encrypt session data during transmission. This protects session information from eavesdropping and tampering attacks.

Implementing these session management best practices helps ensure the security and integrity of user sessions, reducing the risk of session-related vulnerabilities and unauthorized access.

4.4.2 Token-based Authentication

Token-based authentication is a popular approach to enhance security and improve the scalability of authentication systems. It involves issuing tokens to authenticated users, which are then used to authenticate subsequent requests. Tokens can be implemented using various technologies, such as JSON Web Tokens (JWT), OAuth 2.0, or Security Assertion Markup Language (SAML). Here are key considerations for implementing token-based authentication:

Token Generation and Verification: Tokens should be generated securely, using strong cryptographic algorithms and secret keys. Implement token verification mechanisms to ensure the integrity and authenticity of tokens.

Token Expiration: Define token expiration periods to limit their validity and reduce the risk of token misuse. Shorter expiration periods provide enhanced security but require more frequent token renewal.

Revocation and Refreshing: Implement mechanisms for token revocation and refreshing. This allows for invalidating compromised tokens or refreshing expiring tokens without requiring re-authentication.

Token Storage: Tokens should be stored securely on the client-side, using secure storage mechanisms such as HTTP-only cookies or local storage with appropriate security measures. Avoid storing sensitive information within the token payload to minimize the risk of data exposure.

Token Scope and Permissions: Use token scopes and permissions to control the level of access granted to users based on their roles or privileges. Restrict token capabilities to only what is necessary for the user's authorized actions.

Token Encryption: If sensitive information needs to be included in the token payload, consider encrypting the token to protect its contents from unauthorized access or tampering.

Token-based authentication offers several benefits, including statelessness, scalability, and interoperability across different systems. By implementing token-based authentication, organizations can enhance the security and efficiency of authentication processes while providing a seamless user experience.

Securing session management and implementing token-based authentication are crucial steps in building a robust authentication and authorization system. By following these best practices, organizations can mitigate common security vulnerabilities, protect user sessions, and ensure the integrity of user authentication and access control mechanisms.

Chapter 5: Secure Data Storage and Transmission

Welcome to Chapter 5 of "The Secure Coder's Handbook: A Practical Guide to Secure Development." In this chapter, we explore the critical aspects of secure data storage and transmission. By implementing robust measures to protect data at rest and in transit, we can ensure the confidentiality and integrity of sensitive information within our applications.

Data storage security involves safeguarding data while it is at rest, residing in databases, file systems, or other storage mediums. In this chapter, we discuss the importance of encryption in securing data at rest. We explore different encryption techniques, such as symmetric and asymmetric encryption, and examine how to use encryption algorithms and libraries effectively. We also delve into the concept of key management and discuss best practices for storing and protecting encryption keys.

Furthermore, we address the need for secure data sanitization and disposal. When data is no longer needed, it is crucial to properly sanitize or dispose of it to prevent unauthorized access or data leakage. We explore techniques for secure data deletion and discuss the importance of following industry standards and regulations when handling sensitive data.

Data transmission security focuses on protecting data while it is in transit between different systems or across networks. In this chapter, we discuss the significance of secure communication protocols, such as Transport Layer Security (TLS) and Secure Socket Layer (SSL), in ensuring the confidentiality and integrity of data during transmission. We explore best practices for implementing secure communication protocols and examine how to validate server certificates to prevent man-in-the-middle attacks.

We also address common vulnerabilities associated with data storage and transmission, such as SQL injection, cross-site scripting (XSS), and data leakage. We discuss preventive measures, including input validation, output encoding, and secure configuration management, to mitigate these vulnerabilities effectively.

Additionally, we explore the importance of secure data backup and recovery strategies. Regular data backups are essential to protect against data loss and enable system recovery in the event of a security incident or hardware failure. We discuss techniques for securely backing up data and examine considerations for disaster recovery planning.

Throughout this chapter, we emphasize the need to adopt a defense-in-depth approach when securing data storage and transmission. By implementing a combination of encryption, secure communication protocols, input validation, and proper configuration management, we can create multiple layers of protection to safeguard sensitive information.

In the subsequent chapters, we will continue our exploration of secure development practices, including securing web applications, developing secure mobile and IoT applications, and addressing common vulnerabilities. By combining the principles and practices learned in previous chapters with the insights gained from secure data storage and transmission, we will build robust and secure software applications.

So, let's delve into the world of secure data storage and transmission. By embracing these techniques, we can ensure the confidentiality, integrity, and availability of sensitive information within our applications.

5.1 Data Encryption and Key Management

Data encryption plays a vital role in securing sensitive information both at rest and in transit. In this section, we will explore the importance of data encryption and best practices for effective key management.

5.1.1 The Importance of Data Encryption

Data encryption is the process of converting plaintext data into an unreadable format (ciphertext) using cryptographic algorithms. Encryption provides confidentiality and protects data from unauthorized access or disclosure. Whether data is stored in databases, transmitted over networks, or stored in files, encryption ensures that even if it is intercepted or compromised, the data remains unintelligible without the appropriate decryption key.

The benefits of data encryption include:

Confidentiality: Encryption ensures that only authorized parties with the decryption key can access and understand the protected data, safeguarding sensitive information from unauthorized disclosure.

Compliance: Encryption is often a requirement for compliance with various industry standards and data protection regulations. It helps organizations meet legal and regulatory obligations related to the protection of sensitive data.

Data Integrity: Encryption can also provide data integrity by detecting any unauthorized modification or tampering attempts. With the use of encryption algorithms that include integrity checks, organizations can verify the integrity of the encrypted data.

Risk Mitigation: Encrypting sensitive data mitigates the risk of data breaches and reduces the potential impact of unauthorized access. Even if an attacker gains access to the encrypted data, it remains effectively unusable without the decryption key.

Trust and Reputation: Implementing strong encryption measures enhances the trust and confidence of customers and stakeholders. It demonstrates a commitment to protecting their sensitive information, which can positively impact an organization's reputation.

5.1.2 Key Management Best Practices

Effective key management is essential for maintaining the security and integrity of encrypted data. The following best practices should be followed for robust key management:

Key Generation: Use strong and random algorithms to generate encryption keys. Weak or predictable keys can compromise the security of encrypted data. Cryptographically secure random number generators (RNGs) should be employed for key generation.

Key Storage: Protect encryption keys using secure key storage mechanisms. Keys should be stored separately from the encrypted data, limiting access to authorized individuals or systems. Hardware Security Modules (HSMs) or secure key management systems can be used to store and manage encryption keys securely.

Key Distribution: Implement secure key distribution mechanisms when sharing keys between systems or individuals. Use secure channels and protocols to transmit encryption keys, and consider the use of key exchange protocols that provide forward secrecy.

Key Rotation: Periodically rotate encryption keys to enhance security. Key rotation reduces the impact of compromised keys and limits the window of vulnerability in case of a data breach.

Key Revocation: Establish procedures for key revocation in the event of compromised or compromised keys or personnel changes. Revoked keys should be promptly removed from the key management system to prevent their unintended use.

Key Recovery: Implement secure key recovery processes to ensure business continuity and data accessibility in case of key loss or unexpected events. Key recovery should involve proper authentication and authorization to prevent unauthorized access to sensitive data.

Regular Auditing: Conduct regular audits of key management processes and systems to identify potential vulnerabilities or weaknesses. Ensure that key management practices align with industry standards, best practices, and regulatory requirements.

By following these key management best practices, organizations can maintain the confidentiality and integrity of encrypted data, effectively manage encryption keys, and reduce the risk of unauthorized access or data breaches.

Data encryption and key management are critical components of a comprehensive security strategy. By implementing strong encryption measures and adopting robust key management practices, organizations can protect sensitive data, comply with regulations, and enhance overall data security.

5.2 Secure Database Design and SQL Injection Prevention

Securing databases is crucial for protecting sensitive information stored within an organization's systems. In this section, we will explore best practices for secure database design and preventing SQL injection attacks.

5.2.1 Secure Database Design Principles

Secure database design involves implementing measures to protect data integrity, confidentiality, and availability. Here are some essential principles to consider:

Principle of Least Privilege: Follow the principle of least privilege when granting database access permissions. Users should only have the minimum privileges necessary to perform their tasks, reducing the potential impact of unauthorized access or privilege escalation.

Data Classification and Segmentation: Classify data based on its sensitivity level and segment it accordingly. Different levels of access controls should be implemented based on the classification, ensuring that only authorized users can access sensitive data.

Encryption of Sensitive Data: Encrypt sensitive data at rest in the database to prevent unauthorized access. Use strong encryption algorithms and ensure that encryption keys are properly managed and protected.

Regular Database Backups: Implement regular database backups to ensure data availability and facilitate recovery in case of data loss or corruption. Backup files should be securely stored and encrypted to prevent unauthorized access.

Secure Password Storage: Hash passwords using strong and industry-standard hashing algorithms, along with the addition of a unique salt value for each user. Avoid storing passwords in plaintext, as this can lead to their compromise in the event of a data breach.

Secure Configuration: Configure the database server securely by disabling unnecessary services, changing default credentials, and applying necessary security patches and updates. Implement secure network configurations, such as firewall rules, to restrict access to the database server.

5.2.2 SQL Injection Prevention

SQL injection is a common attack vector where malicious actors exploit vulnerabilities in input validation and dynamically constructed SQL queries to execute unauthorized database operations. To prevent SQL injection attacks, follow these best practices:

Parameterized Queries or Prepared Statements: Use parameterized queries or prepared statements with placeholder values instead of dynamically constructing SQL queries. This helps separate the SQL code from user input, preventing malicious input from altering the query structure.

Input Validation and Sanitization: Implement robust input validation and sanitization techniques to ensure that user-supplied data is safe to use in SQL queries. Validate input against expected formats and ranges, and sanitize input by removing or encoding special characters.

Stored Procedures: Utilize stored procedures or parameterized views to encapsulate SQL logic within the database itself. This can help prevent SQL injection by enforcing proper input handling and reducing the risk of dynamic query construction.

Principle of Least Privilege for Database Access: Grant database access permissions based on the principle of least privilege. Restrict access to only the necessary tables, views, and stored procedures, minimizing the potential impact of a successful SQL injection attack.

Regular Security Testing: Conduct regular security assessments and penetration testing to identify and mitigate potential SQL injection vulnerabilities. Use automated tools and manual code review techniques to check for vulnerabilities and validate the effectiveness of implemented security measures.

By following these practices, organizations can mitigate the risk of SQL injection attacks, protect the integrity of their databases, and ensure the confidentiality of sensitive information stored within them.

Secure database design and SQL injection prevention are critical for maintaining the security and trustworthiness of an organization's data storage systems. By incorporating these practices into database development and management processes, organizations can significantly enhance the security posture of their data storage and retrieval mechanisms.

5.3 Secure File Storage and Protection

In addition to databases, organizations often need to store and protect files containing sensitive information. This section focuses on best practices for secure file storage and protection to ensure the confidentiality and integrity of sensitive files.

5.3.1 File Encryption

File encryption is a fundamental measure to protect sensitive files from unauthorized access. By encrypting files, organizations can ensure that even if the files are compromised or accessed without authorization, the data remains encrypted and unreadable. Here are key considerations for file encryption:

Strong Encryption Algorithms: Use strong and industry-recognized encryption algorithms such as Advanced Encryption Standard (AES) to encrypt files.

Ensure that encryption keys are adequately protected and stored separately from the encrypted files.

File-Level Encryption: Encrypt files at the individual file level rather than relying solely on disk or storage-level encryption. This allows for granular control over file encryption and decryption, reducing the potential impact of a data breach.

Key Management: Implement proper key management practices for file encryption. Use secure key storage mechanisms, restrict access to encryption keys, and regularly rotate encryption keys to enhance security.

Secure Transmission of Encrypted Files: If files need to be transmitted over networks or shared externally, ensure that they are encrypted before transmission. Use secure protocols such as Secure File Transfer Protocol (SFTP) or transport layer encryption (e.g., TLS) to protect files during transit.

5.3.2 Access Controls and Authorization

Controlling access to sensitive files is crucial for maintaining their confidentiality and preventing unauthorized modifications. Implementing proper access controls and authorization mechanisms is essential. Consider the following:

Role-Based Access Control (RBAC): Use RBAC to assign specific access permissions to users based on their roles and responsibilities. Limit access to sensitive files to only those users who require it for their job functions.

Access Logging and Monitoring: Implement logging and monitoring mechanisms to track file access activities. This helps detect and investigate any suspicious or unauthorized access attempts.

File Permissions: Set appropriate file permissions at the operating system or file system level to restrict access to authorized users or groups. Regularly review and update file permissions as needed.

File Integrity Verification: Implement file integrity verification mechanisms to ensure that files have not been tampered with or modified without authorization. Hash functions or digital signatures can be used to verify file integrity.

5.3.3 Secure File Transfer and Storage

Secure file transfer and storage are crucial to prevent unauthorized interception or access to sensitive files. Consider the following practices:

Secure File Transfer Protocols: Use secure file transfer protocols such as SFTP or FTPS that encrypt the data during transit. Avoid using unencrypted protocols like FTP, which can expose files to interception and unauthorized access.

Secure File Storage: Store files in secure storage locations with appropriate access controls. This can include encrypted file systems, secure cloud storage services, or on-premises storage solutions protected by physical and logical security measures.

Data Loss Prevention (DLP): Implement DLP measures to prevent the unauthorized transmission or storage of sensitive files. DLP solutions can detect and block the transfer or storage of files that contain sensitive information, helping prevent data leakage.

Regular File Backup: Implement regular file backup procedures to ensure data availability and recoverability. Backup files should be stored securely, following encryption and access control best practices.

By implementing secure file storage and protection practices, organizations can ensure the confidentiality, integrity, and availability of sensitive files. These measures help mitigate the risk of unauthorized access, data breaches, and unauthorized modifications, maintaining the security of valuable information assets.

Secure file storage and protection should be a key aspect of an organization's overall data security strategy, complementing other security measures such as encryption, access controls, and secure transmission protocols.

5.4 Securing Data in Transit: SSL/TLS and Secure Communication Protocols

Securing data during transmission is crucial to protect sensitive information from interception and unauthorized access. In this section, we will explore the importance of SSL/TLS and other secure communication protocols for safeguarding data in transit.

5.4.1 SSL/TLS: The Foundation of Secure Communication

SSL (Secure Socket Layer) and its successor TLS (Transport Layer Security) are cryptographic protocols that establish secure communication channels between clients and servers over networks. They provide encryption, authentication, and data integrity to ensure the confidentiality and integrity of data during transmission.

SSL/TLS utilizes a combination of symmetric and asymmetric encryption algorithms to secure data. The following are key features and components of SSL/TLS:

Encryption: SSL/TLS employs symmetric encryption algorithms to encrypt data. The encryption process ensures that the transmitted information remains confidential and unreadable to unauthorized parties.

Authentication: SSL/TLS utilizes asymmetric encryption and digital certificates to verify the identity of communicating parties. Certificates are issued by trusted Certificate Authorities (CAs) and validate the authenticity of the server and, in some cases, the client.

Data Integrity: SSL/TLS incorporates hashing algorithms to ensure the integrity of transmitted data. Hash functions generate unique checksums that verify whether the data has been tampered with during transit.

Handshake Protocol: The SSL/TLS handshake protocol facilitates the establishment of a secure connection between the client and server. It includes a series of steps for negotiating encryption algorithms, exchanging encryption keys, and verifying certificates.

Cipher Suites: SSL/TLS supports various cipher suites, which are combinations of encryption algorithms and cryptographic parameters. The selection of an appropriate cipher suite ensures the strength of the encryption and the level of security.

5.4.2 Secure Communication Protocols

In addition to SSL/TLS, there are other secure communication protocols that provide protection for specific use cases or network scenarios. Some notable protocols include:

Secure File Transfer Protocol (SFTP): SFTP is a secure protocol designed for secure file transfers over SSH (Secure Shell) connections. It provides encryption and authentication to protect file transfers between clients and servers.

Secure Multipurpose Internet Mail Extensions (S/MIME): S/MIME is an email security protocol that adds encryption and digital signatures to email messages. It ensures the confidentiality and integrity of email content and verifies the identity of senders and recipients.

Internet Protocol Security (IPsec): IPsec is a protocol suite that provides secure communication at the IP layer. It offers encryption, authentication, and integrity protection for IP packets, securing network communications between routers, gateways, and VPNs.

Secure Real-time Transport Protocol (SRTP): SRTP is a security protocol specifically designed to protect real-time voice and video communications. It provides encryption and authentication for VoIP (Voice over IP) and video conferencing applications.

5.4.3 Best Practices for Secure Data Transmission

To ensure secure data transmission, it is essential to follow these best practices:

Implement SSL/TLS: Utilize SSL/TLS to establish secure communication channels for web applications, APIs, and other network services. Configure SSL/TLS settings securely, including using strong cipher suites, disabling weak protocols, and ensuring up-to-date certificate management.

Certificate Management: Properly manage digital certificates, including obtaining certificates from trusted CAs, regularly renewing certificates, and promptly revoking compromised or expired certificates.

Secure Configuration: Configure network devices, servers, and applications to use secure communication protocols by default. Disable insecure protocols, such as older versions of SSL and weak cipher suites, and enforce the use of strong encryption algorithms.

Regular Updates and Patches: Keep SSL/TLS libraries, protocols, and applications up to date with the latest security patches. This helps protect against newly discovered vulnerabilities and ensures the use of the most secure protocols.

Monitoring and Intrusion Detection: Implement network monitoring and intrusion detection systems to detect and respond to potential security incidents or unauthorized access attempts. Monitor SSL/TLS configurations and certificate validity to identify any anomalies or issues.

By implementing SSL/TLS and other secure communication protocols, organizations can protect the confidentiality, integrity, and authenticity of data during transmission. Secure data transmission is crucial for safeguarding sensitive information, maintaining trust with users and customers, and complying with regulatory requirements.

Remember, secure data transmission is just one aspect of overall data protection. It should be combined with secure storage practices, access controls, and other security measures to create a comprehensive data security strategy.

Chapter 6: Securing Web Applications

Welcome to Chapter 6 of "The Secure Coder's Handbook: A Practical Guide to Secure Development." In this chapter, we focus on the specific challenges and techniques involved in securing web applications. With the growing reliance on web-based technologies, it is crucial to implement robust security measures to protect web applications from various threats and vulnerabilities.

We begin by discussing the importance of secure design principles in web application development. By incorporating security considerations from the initial design phase, we can build a solid foundation for secure web applications. We explore concepts such as secure architecture, threat modeling, and secure coding practices specific to web development. Additionally, we discuss the significance of secure configurations and the proper management of web application frameworks and libraries.

Cross-Site Scripting (XSS) and Cross-Site Request Forgery (CSRF) are common vulnerabilities in web applications that can lead to unauthorized data disclosure or malicious actions. In this chapter, we delve into the prevention and mitigation techniques for these vulnerabilities. We discuss input validation, output encoding, and secure session management as effective measures to combat XSS and CSRF attacks.

Next, we explore the importance of secure authentication and session management in web applications. We delve into best practices for implementing strong authentication mechanisms, securely storing user credentials, and protecting user sessions from session hijacking and session fixation attacks. We also discuss the significance of secure password policies, account lockouts, and multi-factor authentication in web application security.

Web application security goes beyond user authentication and authorization. In this chapter, we address the protection of sensitive data in transit and at rest within web applications. We discuss secure communication protocols, such as HTTPS, and explore techniques for encrypting and securely storing sensitive data. Additionally, we examine the importance of secure file handling and the prevention of file upload vulnerabilities.

Another crucial aspect of web application security is the proper handling of user input. In this chapter, we explore techniques for input validation and data sanitization to prevent common vulnerabilities such as SQL injection and command injection. We discuss the significance of parameterized queries, prepared statements, and input validation libraries in mitigating these risks.

Throughout this chapter, we emphasize the importance of ongoing testing and vulnerability scanning in web application security. We discuss the role of penetration testing, code reviews, and automated security tools in identifying and addressing vulnerabilities. Additionally, we explore the significance of secure logging and monitoring in detecting and responding to security incidents.

In conclusion, Chapter 6 equips you with the knowledge and techniques to develop secure web applications. By implementing secure design principles, mitigating vulnerabilities such as XSS and CSRF, ensuring secure authentication and session management, protecting sensitive data, and conducting regular testing, you can enhance the security posture of your web applications and protect them from various threats.

In the subsequent chapters, we will continue our exploration of secure development practices, including developing secure mobile and IoT applications, addressing common vulnerabilities, and establishing a culture of security awareness. By combining the principles and practices learned in previous chapters with the insights gained from securing web applications, you will develop a comprehensive understanding of secure development across various domains.

So, let's dive into the world of securing web applications. By embracing these techniques, you can build resilient and secure web applications that protect both your users and your organization.

6.1 Understanding Web Application Security Threats: Cross-Site Scripting (XSS), Cross-Site Request Forgery (CSRF), etc.

Web applications are a common target for malicious actors seeking to exploit vulnerabilities and gain unauthorized access to sensitive information or disrupt the application's functionality. Understanding web application security threats is crucial for building secure web applications. In this section, we will explore some of the most prevalent web application security threats, including Cross-Site Scripting (XSS), Cross-Site Request Forgery (CSRF), and more.

6.1.1 Cross-Site Scripting (XSS)

Cross-Site Scripting (XSS) is a vulnerability that occurs when a web application fails to properly sanitize user-supplied input, allowing malicious scripts to be injected and executed in users' browsers. XSS attacks can lead to various malicious activities, such as session hijacking, cookie theft, defacement of websites, or the theft of sensitive information. There are three main types of XSS attacks:

Stored XSS: Malicious scripts are permanently stored on the target server, affecting every user who accesses the compromised page or application.

Reflected XSS: Malicious scripts are embedded in URLs or injected into user input fields, and the scripts are reflected back to users as part of the web application's response.

DOM-based XSS: Malicious scripts manipulate the Document Object Model (DOM) of a web page, leading to the execution of unauthorized actions or the theft of sensitive information.

Preventing XSS attacks involves implementing proper input validation and output encoding, utilizing security libraries or frameworks, and following secure coding practices.

6.1.2 Cross-Site Request Forgery (CSRF)

Cross-Site Request Forgery (CSRF) is an attack where an attacker tricks a victim into performing an unwanted action on a web application on which the victim is authenticated. The attack leverages the trust placed in the user's browser by the web application. CSRF attacks can lead to unauthorized actions performed on behalf of the victim, such as changing account settings, making financial transactions, or submitting malicious forms.

To mitigate CSRF attacks, developers should implement measures such as:

CSRF Tokens: Include unique tokens in each user request, which are verified by the server to ensure that the request originated from a legitimate source.

SameSite Cookies: Set the SameSite attribute for cookies to restrict their usage to the same domain, preventing them from being sent in cross-site requests.

Referer Header Validation: Validate the Referer header in incoming requests to ensure that they originated from the expected source.

Multi-Factor Authentication: Require additional authentication factors, such as one-time passwords or biometrics, for critical actions to add an extra layer of security.

6.1.3 Other Web Application Security Threats

In addition to XSS and CSRF, there are several other web application security threats that developers and security professionals should be aware of, including:

SQL Injection: Attackers manipulate user-supplied input to execute unauthorized SQL queries, potentially accessing or modifying sensitive data stored in the application's database.

Remote Code Execution: Vulnerabilities in web applications can allow attackers to execute arbitrary code on the server, leading to complete compromise and control over the application and its data.

File Inclusion Attacks: Attackers exploit insecure file inclusion mechanisms to include malicious files or execute arbitrary code on the server.

Server-Side Request Forgery (SSRF): Attackers manipulate server-side requests to access internal resources or launch attacks against other systems accessible to the server.

XML External Entity (XXE) Attacks: Attackers exploit vulnerabilities in XML parsing to read or exfiltrate sensitive data from the server.

Brute-Force and Credential Stuffing: Attackers attempt to gain unauthorized access by systematically guessing passwords or reusing known username-password combinations.

Understanding these threats and their potential impact is crucial for implementing effective security measures in web applications. Developers should apply secure coding practices, use security libraries and frameworks, regularly update and patch their application dependencies, and conduct thorough security testing and code reviews to identify and remediate vulnerabilities.

By addressing these web application security threats, organizations can significantly reduce the risk of unauthorized access, data breaches, and the compromise of sensitive information. Building secure web applications not only protects users and their data but also helps maintain the reputation and trustworthiness of the application and the organization behind it.

6.2 Input Validation and Filtering in Web Applications

Input validation and filtering are critical components of web application security. They help prevent the exploitation of vulnerabilities that arise from improperly handled user input. In this section, we will explore the importance of input validation and filtering, as well as best practices for implementing them effectively.

6.2.1 The Importance of Input Validation

Web applications rely on user input for various functionalities, such as form submissions, search queries, or data uploads. However, if user input is not properly validated, it can lead to security vulnerabilities, including SQL injection, Cross-Site Scripting (XSS), and command injection.

Input validation involves examining and verifying user-supplied data to ensure it meets the expected format, length, and type. By validating input, developers can identify and reject potentially malicious or malformed data, preventing attacks that exploit vulnerabilities arising from untrusted input.

6.2.2 Best Practices for Input Validation and Filtering

To effectively validate and filter input in web applications, consider the following best practices:

Use Whitelisting: Adopt a whitelist approach by defining acceptable input patterns or values for each input field. Reject any input that does not adhere to these defined patterns or values. This helps prevent various attacks, including XSS and SQL injection.

Validate on the Server-Side: Always validate user input on the server-side, even if there is client-side validation in place. Client-side validation can be bypassed, so server-side validation acts as an additional layer of defense.

Sanitize User Input: Besides validation, input should also be properly sanitized. Sanitization involves removing or encoding potentially harmful characters, such as HTML tags or special characters that could be used for injection attacks.

Use Secure APIs and Libraries: Leverage secure APIs and libraries that provide built-in input validation and filtering mechanisms. These tools can help simplify the process and ensure consistent and effective input validation.

Implement Parameterized Queries: When interacting with databases, use parameterized queries or prepared statements to prevent SQL injection attacks. Parameterization ensures that user-supplied input is treated as data and not executable code.

Regular Expression Validation: Utilize regular expressions to validate input against specific patterns or formats. Regular expressions can be helpful for validating email addresses, phone numbers, or other structured data.

Implement Captcha or ReCAPTCHA: To prevent automated attacks and spam, incorporate Captcha or ReCAPTCHA mechanisms in your web forms. These mechanisms require users to prove their human identity by solving challenges.

Implement Rate Limiting and Anti-Automation Measures: Implement rate limiting techniques to restrict the number of requests from a single IP address within a given time frame. This helps protect against brute-force attacks and other automated threats.

Perform Input Length Validation: Validate the length of input to prevent buffer overflow or denial-of-service attacks. Limit the length of input based on the specific requirements of each field.

Regularly Update and Patch Dependencies: Keep all libraries, frameworks, and plugins used in your web application up to date. Developers often release updates to address security vulnerabilities, and staying current is crucial for maintaining a secure application.

By following these best practices, web developers can significantly reduce the risk of vulnerabilities arising from improper input handling. Input validation and filtering play a vital role in ensuring the security and integrity of web applications, protecting against various types of attacks that target user input.

Remember, input validation should be considered just one aspect of a comprehensive web application security strategy. It should be complemented by other security measures, such as secure coding practices, secure configuration management, and regular security testing, to create a robust defense against potential threats.

6.3 Secure Session Handling and Cookie Security

Web applications often utilize sessions and cookies to maintain user state and provide a personalized experience. However, if session handling and cookie security are not implemented properly, it can lead to severe security vulnerabilities, such as session hijacking, session fixation, and information leakage. In this section, we will explore the importance of secure session handling and cookie security, along with best practices for mitigating associated risks.

6.3.1 Importance of Secure Session Handling

Sessions allow web applications to maintain user state across multiple requests. They enable the application to identify and authenticate users, store session-related data, and ensure a seamless browsing experience. However, it is crucial to handle sessions securely to prevent unauthorized access and protect user privacy.

Secure session handling involves implementing measures to ensure the confidentiality, integrity, and uniqueness of session identifiers. It also involves proper session management, including session creation, expiration, and termination, to mitigate the risk of session-related attacks.

6.3.2 Best Practices for Secure Session Handling and Cookie Security

To ensure secure session handling and cookie security in web applications, consider the following best practices:

Use Secure and HTTP-only Cookies: Set the "secure" and "HTTP-only" attributes for cookies. The "secure" attribute ensures that cookies are only transmitted over secure HTTPS connections, while the "HTTP-only" attribute prevents client-side scripts from accessing cookies, reducing the risk of session theft through cross-site scripting (XSS) attacks.

Implement Session Expiration: Set appropriate session expiration times to limit the duration of active sessions. This reduces the window of opportunity for session hijacking and helps ensure that inactive sessions are terminated automatically.

Regenerate Session IDs: Generate new session IDs upon successful authentication, session privilege changes, or any other sensitive operations. This prevents session fixation attacks, where an attacker forces a known session ID onto a victim.

Implement Session Invalidation: Invalidate or destroy sessions after users log out or after a specific period of inactivity. Proper session invalidation ensures that revoked or expired sessions cannot be reused or hijacked.

Encrypt Session Data: If sensitive data needs to be stored in sessions, ensure it is properly encrypted to protect against unauthorized access. Use strong encryption algorithms and securely manage encryption keys.

Implement Secure Transport Layer: Ensure that all communications, including session handling and cookie exchange, are performed over a secure HTTPS connection. HTTPS encrypts data in transit, preventing interception and tampering.

Perform Strict Session Validation: Validate session identifiers on every request to ensure they are valid, active, and associated with the authenticated user. Reject requests with invalid or expired session IDs.

Protect Against Cross-Site Request Forgery (CSRF): Implement CSRF protection mechanisms, such as anti-CSRF tokens, to prevent attackers from exploiting authenticated user sessions to perform unauthorized actions.

Monitor and Detect Anomalies: Implement session monitoring and anomaly detection mechanisms to identify suspicious activities, such as simultaneous logins from different locations or unusual session lifetimes.

Educate Users on Session Security: Provide guidance to users on maintaining session security, such as advising them not to share their session identifiers or login credentials and encouraging them to log out properly.

By adhering to these best practices, web application developers can significantly enhance session security and mitigate the risk of session-related attacks. Secure session handling and cookie security are crucial for protecting user identities, maintaining privacy, and ensuring a trustworthy user experience.

Remember, session handling is just one aspect of web application security. It should be complemented by other security measures, such as secure authentication, input validation, and secure coding practices, to create a comprehensive security posture for web applications.

6.4 Securing Web APIs: Authentication, Authorization, and Input Validation

Web APIs (Application Programming Interfaces) have become a fundamental component of modern web applications, enabling seamless integration with other systems and services. However, the exposure of APIs to the internet introduces additional security considerations. In this section, we will explore the importance of securing web APIs, focusing on authentication, authorization, and input validation.

6.4.1 Authentication in Web APIs

Authentication is the process of verifying the identity of a user or system accessing an API. Proper authentication ensures that only authorized entities can access and interact with sensitive data or perform restricted operations. When securing web APIs, consider the following authentication mechanisms:

API Keys: Assign unique API keys to each authorized client or application. API keys act as credentials for accessing the API and can be included in requests as headers or query parameters.

Token-Based Authentication: Implement token-based authentication mechanisms such as JSON Web Tokens (JWT) or OAuth. Clients obtain tokens upon successful authentication, which they include in subsequent requests to authenticate themselves.

OAuth and OpenID Connect: Leverage OAuth and OpenID Connect protocols for delegated authentication and authorization. These protocols enable users to authenticate through trusted identity providers, reducing the risk of storing and managing sensitive user credentials.

Mutual TLS (Transport Layer Security): Implement Mutual TLS to establish a secure, authenticated connection between clients and the API server. This approach relies on client and server certificates to ensure the authenticity and integrity of the communication.

Biometric Authentication: For certain use cases, consider integrating biometric authentication mechanisms, such as fingerprint or facial recognition, to enhance security and user experience.

6.4.2 Authorization in Web APIs

Authorization determines what actions and resources a user or system can access within an API. It ensures that authenticated entities have the necessary permissions to perform specific operations. Consider the following practices for secure API authorization:

Role-Based Access Control (RBAC): Implement RBAC to assign roles to users or systems and define the permissions associated with each role. Users are then granted access based on their assigned roles.

Attribute-Based Access Control (ABAC): Employ ABAC to define access policies based on attributes of the user, resource, or environment. ABAC provides more granular control over access by considering multiple attributes and conditions.

API Scopes: Use API scopes to limit access to specific resources or actions within the API. Each authenticated entity is granted scopes based on their authorization level, ensuring they only have access to the necessary functionalities.

Fine-Grained Authorization: Implement fine-grained authorization checks at the API endpoints to ensure that clients can only access the resources they are authorized to access. Validate permissions and ownership before allowing actions on sensitive data.

Access Token Validation: Perform proper validation of access tokens and enforce authorization checks at the API level. Validate the integrity and authenticity of access tokens, and ensure they have not expired or been tampered with.

6.4.3 Input Validation and Security

Input validation is essential for securing web APIs as it helps prevent vulnerabilities, such as injection attacks, data exposure, and unintended access.

Consider the following best practices for input validation and security in web APIs:

Input Sanitization: Implement input sanitization to remove or escape potentially dangerous characters from user-supplied input. Use well-tested libraries or frameworks to handle input sanitization effectively.

Parameterized Queries: Use parameterized queries or prepared statements to prevent SQL injection attacks when interacting with databases. Parameterization ensures that user input is treated as data, rather than executable code.

Validate and Normalize Input: Validate and enforce data types, lengths, and formats of input parameters. Normalize input to ensure consistent representation and prevent encoding-related vulnerabilities.

Rate Limiting and Throttling: Implement rate limiting and throttling mechanisms to prevent abusive or malicious usage of the API. Limit the number of requests from a single client or IP address within a specified time period.

Input Filtering and Whitelisting: Filter and whitelist user input to allow only expected characters or patterns. Reject any input that does not conform to the predefined whitelist.

Content-Type Validation: Validate and enforce the Content-Type header to ensure that the data being sent matches the expected format. This helps prevent content-type-related attacks, such as XML or JSON injections.

Regularly Update and Patch Dependencies: Keep all libraries, frameworks, and dependencies up to date. Developers often release updates to address security vulnerabilities, and staying current is crucial for maintaining a secure API.

By implementing robust authentication, authorization, and input validation mechanisms, developers can enhance the security of their web APIs. These practices help protect sensitive data, prevent unauthorized access, and mitigate the risk of common API security vulnerabilities.

Remember, securing web APIs is an ongoing process that requires continuous monitoring, threat modeling, and security testing. Stay informed about the latest security best practices and emerging threats to ensure that your APIs remain resilient against evolving security risks.

Chapter 7: Secure Development for Mobile and IoT Applications

Welcome to Chapter 7 of "The Secure Coder's Handbook: A Practical Guide to Secure Development." In this chapter, we shift our focus to the unique challenges and considerations involved in developing secure mobile and Internet of Things (IoT) applications. With the increasing popularity and proliferation of mobile devices and IoT devices, it is crucial to implement robust security measures to protect these applications and the sensitive data they handle.

We begin by discussing the specific security challenges faced by mobile applications. Mobile platforms introduce unique risks, including data leakage, insecure storage, and unauthorized access to device features. We explore techniques for securing mobile application code, including secure coding practices and the use of application hardening and obfuscation techniques. We also delve into secure storage mechanisms for sensitive data on mobile devices, such as encryption and secure key management.

Next, we explore the importance of secure communication in mobile applications. We discuss secure communication protocols, such as Transport Layer Security (TLS), and examine techniques for validating server certificates and preventing man-in-the-middle attacks. Additionally, we address secure authentication and authorization mechanisms specific to mobile applications, considering factors such as user experience, device capabilities, and potential risks.

Mobile applications often rely on backend services and APIs for data exchange. In this chapter, we discuss the significance of secure API design and protection against common vulnerabilities, such as injection attacks and insecure data transmission. We explore techniques such as input validation, output encoding, and API authentication and authorization to ensure the security of data exchange between mobile applications and backend services.

Furthermore, we explore the security considerations unique to IoT applications. IoT devices introduce a new layer of complexity, including firmware security, secure communication protocols, and secure device management. We discuss best practices for securing IoT devices, including secure bootstrapping, device authentication, and secure over-the-air (OTA) updates. We also address the importance of secure communication between IoT devices and backend systems, including the use of protocols such as MQTT and CoAP.

In both mobile and IoT applications, data privacy and user consent are paramount. We discuss the significance of privacy policies, user consent mechanisms, and data anonymization techniques in ensuring the privacy of user data. We also explore the implications of regulatory frameworks, such as the General Data Protection Regulation (GDPR), and discuss how to align development practices with privacy requirements.

Throughout this chapter, we emphasize the importance of ongoing vulnerability assessments and security testing for mobile and IoT applications. We discuss the role of penetration testing, code reviews, and security audits in identifying vulnerabilities and mitigating risks. Additionally, we explore the significance of implementing secure coding practices, conducting threat modeling, and fostering a security-aware development culture within mobile and IoT development teams.

In conclusion, Chapter 7 equips you with the knowledge and techniques to develop secure mobile and IoT applications. By addressing the unique challenges and risks associated with these domains, implementing secure coding practices, securing data communication, and considering privacy and regulatory requirements, you can build applications that protect both users and their sensitive data.

In the subsequent chapters, we will continue our exploration of secure development practices, including addressing common vulnerabilities, secure deployment and operations, and establishing a culture of security awareness. By combining the principles and practices learned in previous chapters with the insights gained from securing mobile and IoT applications, you will develop a comprehensive understanding of secure development across various domains.

So, let's delve into the world of secure development for mobile and IoT applications. By embracing these techniques, you can build resilient and secure applications that leverage the power of mobile and IoT technologies while safeguarding user privacy and data.

7.1 Mobile Application Security Best Practices

Mobile applications have become an integral part of our daily lives, offering convenience and functionality on the go. However, the sensitive data and functionalities they handle make them attractive targets for attackers. To ensure the security of mobile applications, developers must adhere to best practices that address the unique challenges and vulnerabilities associated with mobile environments.

In this section, we will explore key mobile application security best practices.

Secure Code Practices: Apply secure coding principles to mobile application development. Use secure coding practices, such as input validation, output encoding, secure storage, and secure communication, to prevent common vulnerabilities like injection attacks, cross-site scripting (XSS), and data leakage.

Secure Authentication and Authorization: Implement strong authentication mechanisms, such as biometrics, multi-factor authentication, or token-based authentication, to ensure the proper identification and authorization of users. Use secure protocols and encryption techniques for transmitting authentication data.

Secure Data Storage: Protect sensitive data stored on the mobile device by utilizing secure storage mechanisms, such as encrypting data at rest, using strong encryption algorithms, and securely managing encryption keys. Avoid storing sensitive information unnecessarily.

Secure Network Communication: Employ secure network communication protocols, such as HTTPS, to encrypt data transmitted between the mobile application and backend servers. Validate server certificates to prevent man-in-the-middle attacks.

Avoid transmitting sensitive data over unsecured or public networks.

Input Validation and Output Encoding: Implement robust input validation to prevent injection attacks and enforce data integrity. Use output encoding techniques to protect against cross-site scripting (XSS) vulnerabilities, ensuring that user-supplied data is properly sanitized before being displayed or processed.

Secure Session Management: Implement secure session handling mechanisms in mobile applications to protect against session hijacking and session fixation attacks. Generate strong and unique session identifiers, enforce session expiration, and ensure proper session invalidation upon logout or app termination.

Code Obfuscation: Apply code obfuscation techniques to make reverse engineering and code analysis more challenging for attackers. Obfuscation can help protect sensitive algorithms, API keys, and other critical components of the application.

Secure Offline Storage: If the application requires offline storage of sensitive data, employ encryption and access control mechanisms to safeguard the data stored locally on the device. Use secure storage containers or hardware-backed encryption where available.

User Input Protection: Implement input protection mechanisms to guard against user input tampering or injection attacks. Validate and sanitize user input before processing it to prevent manipulation or exploitation of application logic.

Regular Updates and Patch Management: Continuously update the mobile application to address security vulnerabilities, bug fixes, and performance improvements. Promptly address reported security issues and vulnerabilities, and ensure a seamless update process for users.

User Education and Awareness: Educate users about mobile application security best practices, such as avoiding downloading apps from unofficial sources, being cautious with granting app permissions, and regularly updating their mobile operating system and applications.

Security Testing and Vulnerability Assessments: Conduct comprehensive security testing, including penetration testing and vulnerability assessments, to identify and address potential security weaknesses in the application. Regularly test the application against emerging threats and security standards.

By following these mobile application security best practices, developers can significantly reduce the risk of security breaches, data leaks, and unauthorized access to sensitive information. Remember that security is an ongoing process, and it requires continuous monitoring, proactive measures, and staying updated with the latest security trends and vulnerabilities in the mobile landscape.

7.2 Securing Data Storage and Encryption in Mobile Applications

Mobile applications often handle sensitive user data, including personal information, login credentials, financial details, and more. Securing this data is of utmost importance to protect users' privacy and prevent unauthorized access. In this section, we will explore best practices for securing data storage and encryption in mobile applications.

Data Classification: Start by classifying the data your mobile application handles. Identify which data is considered sensitive or confidential, and prioritize its protection. This will help you determine the appropriate security measures to apply.

Secure Local Data Storage: Mobile devices store data locally, which poses risks if the data is not adequately protected. Apply encryption to sensitive data stored on the device, such as user credentials, personal information, or any other sensitive data.

Leverage platform-specific encryption mechanisms and libraries to encrypt data at rest.

Key Management: Implement a robust key management strategy to securely store encryption keys used for data protection. Avoid hardcoding keys within the application code and consider leveraging platform-specific secure storage for keys or utilizing hardware-backed encryption.

Secure Credential Storage: Mobile applications often require users to log in using credentials. Avoid storing credentials in plain text or using weak encryption algorithms. Instead, use strong, one-way hashing algorithms like bcrypt or PBKDF2 to securely store passwords. Additionally, consider implementing secure authentication mechanisms such as biometrics or token-based authentication.

Transport Layer Security (TLS): Ensure that all communication between the mobile application and backend servers is encrypted using secure communication protocols like HTTPS. Validate server certificates to prevent man-in-the-middle attacks.

Secure Data Transmission: When transmitting sensitive data over the network, encrypt it to prevent unauthorized interception or tampering. Leverage encryption protocols such as SSL/TLS to establish secure communication channels between the mobile application and backend servers.

Secure Database Integration: If your mobile application interacts with a backend database, implement secure integration practices. Utilize secure APIs and enforce strong authentication and authorization mechanisms to protect against unauthorized access or data manipulation.

Data Minimization: Minimize the amount of data stored on the device and transmitted over the network. Only collect and retain the data necessary for the application's functionality. Implement data anonymization techniques where possible to further protect user privacy.

Secure Data Removal: When sensitive data is no longer required, ensure proper removal from the device's storage. Implement secure deletion techniques to prevent data remnants from being recovered. This is particularly important when handling user data or sensitive information.

Security Testing: Regularly perform security testing and vulnerability assessments on your mobile application to identify potential security weaknesses. This includes testing for storage-related vulnerabilities such as insecure data storage, weak encryption, or insecure key management.

Compliance with Privacy Regulations: Be aware of and comply with applicable privacy regulations, such as the General Data Protection Regulation (GDPR) or the California Consumer Privacy Act (CCPA). Understand the data protection requirements and implement the necessary security measures to meet the compliance standards.

By implementing these best practices, mobile application developers can significantly enhance the security of data storage and encryption in their applications. Prioritize data protection, leverage platform-specific security features, and regularly assess and update security measures to stay ahead of emerging threats. Remember, protecting user data is not only a legal and ethical responsibility but also crucial for maintaining user trust and ensuring the long-term success of your mobile application.

7.3 Securing Network Communication in Mobile Apps

In today's interconnected world, mobile applications heavily rely on network communication to interact with backend servers, exchange data, and provide various services. However, this dependence on network communication introduces potential security risks and vulnerabilities. In this section, we will explore best practices for securing network communication in mobile applications.

Use Secure Protocols: Ensure that all network communication between the mobile application and backend servers is encrypted using secure protocols such as HTTPS. HTTPS provides a secure channel by encrypting data in transit and verifying the server's identity through SSL/TLS certificates.

Certificate Validation: Implement proper certificate validation to prevent man-in-the-middle attacks. Verify the server's SSL/TLS certificate during the initial handshake and ensure that it is valid, trusted, and issued by a recognized certificate authority (CA).

Certificate Pinning: Consider implementing certificate pinning, which involves associating a specific server certificate or its public key with your mobile application. By pinning the certificate, you can ensure that your application only communicates with the intended server and helps protect against fraudulent certificates.

Server-Side Security Configuration: Configure your backend servers to enforce secure communication practices. This includes disabling outdated or weak encryption protocols and algorithms, enabling secure cipher suites, and implementing strong server-side security configurations.

Secure Data Transmission: Encrypt sensitive data transmitted over the network to prevent unauthorized interception or tampering. Utilize encryption protocols such as SSL/TLS to establish secure communication channels between the mobile application and backend servers.

Implement Two-Factor Authentication (2FA): Consider implementing two-factor authentication for user authentication. This adds an extra layer of security by requiring users to provide a second form of verification, such as a one-time password (OTP) or biometric authentication, in addition to their credentials.

Implement Secure Authentication Mechanisms: Avoid sending sensitive information, such as passwords or authentication tokens, in plain text over the network. Utilize secure authentication mechanisms like OAuth, OpenID Connect, or token-based authentication to protect user credentials during authentication.

Securely Handle Session Tokens: If your mobile application uses session tokens for authentication, ensure they are securely transmitted and stored. Use secure transport mechanisms, such as HTTPS, for transmitting session tokens and employ secure storage practices on the device to protect against session hijacking or token leakage.

Protect against Replay Attacks: Implement mechanisms to prevent replay attacks, where an attacker intercepts and replays a legitimate network request. Use techniques such as request timestamp validation, nonces, or cryptographic challenges to ensure that each request is fresh and not a replayed request.

Regularly Update SSL/TLS Libraries: Keep the SSL/TLS libraries used in your mobile application up to date. Developers often release updates to address security vulnerabilities, and staying current with the latest versions helps ensure that your application benefits from the latest security patches and improvements.

Security Testing: Perform regular security testing, including penetration testing and vulnerability assessments, to identify any security weaknesses in your mobile application's network communication. This helps uncover potential vulnerabilities and provides an opportunity to address them proactively.

Implement Network Security Controls: Leverage platform-specific network security controls and features provided by the mobile operating system. These controls can help enforce secure communication practices, restrict network access, and prevent unauthorized connections.

By following these best practices, mobile application developers can enhance the security of network communication and mitigate the risks associated with transmitting data over the network. Prioritize secure protocols, implement encryption, validate certificates, and regularly assess and update security measures to stay ahead of potential threats. Remember, securing network communication is essential to protect user data, maintain the integrity of your mobile application, and preserve user trust in your product.

7.4 IoT Application Security: Authentication, Encryption, and Secure Protocols

With the proliferation of Internet of Things (IoT) devices, the need for robust security measures in IoT applications has become paramount. IoT devices often collect and transmit sensitive data, making them attractive targets for attackers. In this section, we will explore best practices for securing IoT applications, focusing on authentication, encryption, and the use of secure protocols.

Secure Authentication: Implement strong authentication mechanisms for IoT devices to ensure that only authorized entities can access and control them. This can include methods such as unique device credentials, certificates, or two-factor authentication. Avoid using default or weak credentials, and enforce strong password policies.

Secure Communication Protocols: Use secure communication protocols to transmit data between IoT devices and backend systems. Protocols such as MQTT (Message Queuing Telemetry Transport) or HTTPS (Hypertext Transfer Protocol Secure) provide encryption and authentication mechanisms, ensuring secure data transmission.

Encryption of Data in Transit: Encrypt data transmitted between IoT devices and backend systems to prevent unauthorized interception or tampering. Apply encryption techniques such as SSL/TLS (Secure Sockets Layer/Transport Layer Security) to establish secure communication channels.

Encryption of Data at Rest: Protect sensitive data stored on IoT devices by encrypting it at rest. This prevents unauthorized access to data even if the device is compromised. Use strong encryption algorithms and ensure secure key management practices to safeguard the encryption keys.

Device Identity and Authentication: Each IoT device should have a unique identity that can be verified during the authentication process. This ensures that only legitimate devices can communicate with the backend systems. Consider using device certificates or other secure identity mechanisms.

Secure Over-the-Air (OTA) Updates: Implement secure OTA update mechanisms to ensure that IoT devices receive firmware updates and security patches in a secure manner. Use secure protocols and cryptographic techniques to verify the authenticity and integrity of updates before installation.

Secure Configuration: Ensure that IoT devices are securely configured, with appropriate security settings applied. This includes disabling unnecessary services, changing default credentials, and implementing secure network configurations to prevent unauthorized access.

Physical Security Measures: Consider physical security measures to protect IoT devices from physical tampering or unauthorized access. This can include tamper-evident packaging, secure enclosure design, or device location restrictions to minimize physical risks.

Continuous Monitoring and Intrusion Detection: Implement monitoring and intrusion detection mechanisms to detect and respond to potential security breaches or unauthorized activities. This can include anomaly detection, behavior analysis, or network traffic monitoring to identify suspicious activities.

Privacy Considerations: IoT applications often involve the collection and processing of personal data. Ensure compliance with privacy regulations and consider privacy by design principles. Implement data minimization techniques, secure data handling practices, and provide transparent privacy policies to users.

Security Testing: Conduct comprehensive security testing and vulnerability assessments for IoT applications. This includes penetration testing, code review, and testing for common IoT vulnerabilities such as insecure communication, weak authentication, or insufficient encryption.

Vendor and Supply Chain Security: Evaluate the security practices of IoT device vendors and ensure that they follow secure development processes. Verify the integrity and security of third-party components or libraries used in your IoT application to prevent potential vulnerabilities.

By implementing these best practices, IoT application developers can enhance the security of their systems and protect sensitive data from unauthorized access or tampering. Secure authentication, encryption, and the use of secure protocols are crucial in safeguarding IoT applications and building user trust. Remember that IoT security is an ongoing process, requiring continuous monitoring, updates, and proactive measures to address emerging threats in the dynamic IoT landscape.

7.5 Secure Firmware Development for IoT Devices

Firmware plays a critical role in the functioning of IoT devices, as it controls their operation and behavior. However, insecure firmware can introduce significant vulnerabilities and compromise the security of the entire IoT ecosystem. In this section, we will explore best practices for secure firmware development for IoT devices.

Secure Boot Process: Implement a secure boot process to ensure that only trusted firmware can be loaded and executed on the IoT device. Use cryptographic techniques, such as digital signatures or secure bootloaders, to verify the authenticity and integrity of firmware images during the boot process.

Firmware Integrity Protection: Protect the integrity of the firmware throughout its lifecycle. Use cryptographic techniques, such as hash functions or digital signatures, to verify the integrity of the firmware at various stages, including during storage, transit, and installation.

Code Review and Static Analysis: Perform thorough code review and static analysis of the firmware codebase to identify potential security vulnerabilities, such as buffer overflows, input validation issues, or insecure cryptographic implementations. Use automated tools and manual review processes to uncover security flaws.

Secure Coding Practices: Adhere to secure coding practices during firmware development. Follow principles such as input validation, output encoding, secure memory management, and secure data handling to prevent common vulnerabilities like injection attacks or buffer overflows.

Secure Firmware Updates: Implement secure firmware update mechanisms to ensure that IoT devices can receive and install updates in a secure and reliable manner. Use secure protocols, digital signatures, and encryption to protect firmware updates from tampering or unauthorized modifications.

Least Privilege Principle: Apply the principle of least privilege to firmware development. Grant only the necessary permissions and privileges to the firmware components, processes, and services to minimize the potential impact of a compromise or vulnerability.

Secure Communication Interfaces: Implement secure communication interfaces for firmware updates, configuration management, and other interactions with the IoT device. Use secure protocols, encryption, and authentication mechanisms to protect data transmitted over these interfaces.

Encryption and Secure Storage: If the IoT device stores sensitive data or configuration information, ensure that it is encrypted and securely stored. Use strong encryption algorithms, secure key management practices, and appropriate access control mechanisms to protect stored data.

Vulnerability Management: Establish a vulnerability management process for firmware development. Stay informed about emerging security vulnerabilities and proactively address them through patches, updates, or firmware revisions. Monitor security advisories and maintain a mechanism for receiving and addressing vulnerability reports.

Secure Development Lifecycle: Incorporate secure development practices into the firmware development lifecycle. This includes security requirements analysis, threat modeling, secure design, implementation, testing, and ongoing security maintenance. Ensure that security is considered at each stage of the development process.

Hardware Security Measures: Collaborate with hardware designers to implement appropriate hardware security measures that complement the firmware security. This can include hardware-based encryption, secure storage elements, or secure microcontrollers to enhance overall system security.

Compliance and Certification: Understand and comply with relevant industry standards, security guidelines, and regulatory requirements applicable to IoT devices. Consider seeking certifications or undergoing security assessments to demonstrate the security robustness of your firmware.

By following these best practices, firmware developers can significantly enhance the security of IoT devices. Secure boot processes, integrity protection, code review, secure coding practices, and secure update mechanisms all contribute to building a more resilient and secure firmware infrastructure. Remember that secure firmware development is an ongoing effort, requiring constant vigilance and a commitment to staying up-to-date with emerging threats and best practices.

"The Secure Coder's Handbook: A Practical Guide to Secure Development" serves as a comprehensive resource for developers, engineers, and software professionals looking to enhance their understanding of secure coding practices. Throughout this book, we have explored the fundamental principles, best practices, and techniques necessary to build robust and secure applications.

In the first chapter, we emphasized the importance of integrating security into the development process from the outset. By recognizing the impact of insecure code on applications and systems, we were able to establish a strong foundation for the subsequent chapters. Understanding the potential consequences of security vulnerabilities motivates us to prioritize secure coding practices as an essential component of our development workflows.

Chapter 2 guided us through the core principles and best practices of secure coding. We delved into input validation, output encoding, error handling, and secure configuration management. By implementing these practices, we significantly reduce the risk of common vulnerabilities, such as injection attacks, buffer overflows, and cross-site scripting. Additionally, we explored the value of adhering to secure coding standards and frameworks, which provide guidelines for maintaining code integrity and security.

Threat modeling and risk assessment took center stage in Chapter 3. We learned how to identify potential security risks, analyze their impact and likelihood, and prioritize and mitigate risks accordingly. This proactive approach ensures that our resources are allocated effectively, targeting the areas of greatest vulnerability. By conducting security code reviews and audits, we are able to continually assess and enhance the security of our codebase.

Chapter 4 focused on secure authentication and authorization mechanisms. We examined various techniques, such as multi-factor authentication, biometrics, and secure session management, to ensure that only authorized individuals can access sensitive resources. Furthermore, we explored different authorization models, such as role-based and attribute-based access control, to implement robust access control mechanisms. By understanding the importance of strong authentication and granular authorization, we safeguard our applications against unauthorized access and potential data breaches.

Securing data throughout its lifecycle was the subject of Chapter 5. Encryption and hashing techniques were explored in detail, enabling us to protect sensitive data stored in databases, files, and other storage mediums. Additionally, we discussed the significance of secure data transmission, emphasizing the use of encryption and secure communication protocols to safeguard data in transit. By employing these practices, we ensure the confidentiality and integrity of our users' data.

Web applications present unique challenges due to their exposure to the public internet. Chapter 6 addressed these challenges head-on, exploring common web application vulnerabilities, including cross-site scripting (XSS) and cross-site request forgery (CSRF). Through secure coding practices, input validation, and output encoding, we can minimize the risk of exploitation and protect user data from malicious attacks. By staying informed about emerging threats and employing effective countermeasures, we fortify our web applications against potential vulnerabilities.

The final chapter, Chapter 7, turned our attention to secure development practices for mobile and IoT applications. With the proliferation of smartphones and connected devices, ensuring the security of these platforms has become crucial. We discussed the unique challenges and vulnerabilities associated with mobile and IoT applications, including securing data storage, network communication, and firmware development. By implementing secure coding practices specifically tailored to these environments, we mitigate the risks and protect the integrity and privacy of user data.

"The Secure Coder's Handbook: A Practical Guide to Secure Development" aims to empower developers with the knowledge and skills to write secure code. By adhering to the principles and practices outlined in this book, we can significantly reduce the likelihood of security breaches, protect sensitive information, and uphold the trust of our users and stakeholders.

Security is an ongoing commitment that requires constant vigilance and adaptation to emerging threats. By adopting a security-conscious mindset and staying updated on the evolving landscape of security practices, we can continue to improve our secure coding abilities. Remember, secure development is not an isolated endeavor but a collective effort to build a safer digital world.

As we conclude our journey through this handbook, I encourage you to embrace the knowledge and insights gained here and apply them in your day-to-day development activities. By prioritizing security, you contribute to the overall resilience of the digital ecosystem. Together, let us strive for secure, reliable, and trustworthy software applications.

Thank you for embarking on this journey with "The Secure Coder's Handbook: A Practical Guide to Secure Development." May your code always be secure and your applications fortified against the ever-evolving landscape of cyber threats.

Happy coding and secure development!

www.ingramcontent.com/pod-product-compliance
Lightning Source LLC
Chambersburg PA
CBHW060838220526
45466CB00003B/1150